THE SEXUAL REVOLUTION

Bishop Peter J. Elliott

THE SEXUAL REVOLUTION

History—Ideology—Power

IGNATIUS PRESS   SAN FRANCISCO

First published, under the same title in Australia, by
Freedom Publishing Books, Bayswater, Victoria
© 2020 by Peter J. Elliott
All rights reserved

Nihil Obstat: Reverend Dr. Cameron Forbes, STD, Diocesan Censor

Imprimatur: + Very Reverend Joseph Caddy, AM Lic. Soc.Sci. VG
Vicar General, Archdiocese of Melbourne
October 12, 2020

Art and cover design by Enrique J. Aguilar

Published in 2023 by Ignatius Press, San Francisco
Published by arrangement with Freedom Publishing Books Pty Ltd
Foreword and Introduction © 2023 by Ignatius Press, San Francisco
All rights reserved
ISBN 978-1-62164-575-7 (PB)
ISBN 978-1-64229-216-9 (e-Book)
Library of Congress Control Number 2022941264
Printed in the United States of America ∞

CONTENTS

FOREWORD

Our society has been significantly changed by the sexual revolution that has taken place over the past fifty years. It has been growing in intensity and appears unstoppable. Moral principles we once thought were clear and evident absolutes in our culture—based on Judeo-Christian beliefs—have one by one been rejected. Legislation and public policy that promoted and defended human flourishing are now subject to persistent challenge.

Change in sexual mores has become the constant. What was once considered extreme with regard to human sexuality and sexual identity is now a commonplace idea, such as the disturbing fad of gender fluidity. Legislative changes that endorse radical new ways of seeing human sexual identity have passed relatively easily through the parliaments. These changes create a legislative fiction, because we know this is not good and cannot be good for our society.

We once thought that there were certain basic truths about the human person that would never be challenged. The notion of only two sexes oriented to marriage as the life-long relationship of sexual fidelity between a man and a woman is no longer accepted by many in our society. We are expected to accept all sorts of alternatives. We understood marriage and family as the sound foundation to society and the ground upon which individuals could fully flourish as human beings. This is all being pushed aside, and we feel the pressure to accept these changes.

Increasingly, we are also seeing attempts to restrict individuals and organizations from expressing what were once viewed as time-honored truths about the human person. Freedom of speech and conscience are under significant attack. The cries for tolerance by some minority groups quickly changes to a demand for total endorsement of their identity and agenda. At times, it seems like we are facing a tsunami of social change over which we have no influence. We are being swept away by forces far beyond our capacity to match.

Bishop Elliott has done us a great service in outlining the various elements that have shaped this extraordinary period of social change. In an historical survey that is fast paced and informative, he has identified key players and movements that have largely brought about these social changes. He provides us with an invaluable historical study of the sexual revolution that has so shaped the path of Western, indeed, global culture over the past fifty years.

We can feel powerless in the face of such rapid change. However, as Bishop Elliott points out, the Christian is one who has hope. Christianity declares that God has not abandoned sinful humanity. Indeed, God's intervention into human history has inaugurated the era of truth and grace.

In the end, we know that human nature was created good by God. Built into our nature is a desire for truth, goodness, and beauty. These transcendentals may be difficult to grasp in an age so disfigured by ideology and false ideas, but they cannot be eliminated from human nature. The Natural Law may be dismissed and ridiculed, but it still remains because it has been placed there by a wise Creator. We are as God has made us. We are made in the image and likeness of God, and there lies within each human being a desire for God and what He has intended for us.

Whatever false ideas are generated and at times seem to dominate our society, a desire for the three transcendentals— truth, goodness, and beauty—will eventually rise afresh in the hearts not only of believers but in anyone, for they are what lies in the depths of every human heart.

Drawing on a lifetime of involvement promoting the Church's mission on marriage and family life, including serving with the Pontifical Council for the Family, Bishop Elliott has provided an invaluable analysis of the sexual revolution, and he offers a range of practical recommendations that can act as an antidote to the poison that is corrupting human society.

Reading this account of the sexual revolution may be a source of dismay, but Christian hope never fades.

Most Rev. Julian Porteous
Archbishop of Hobart

INTRODUCTION

Some readers may be surprised that a Catholic bishop has ventured into such a minefield as the "sexual revolution". I wrote this book to honor the people's right to be informed about what is happening in our society, to help them identify and understand the powerful and wealthy forces at work in the sexual revolution.

It is only in the context of what is happening in the twenty-first century, the wider social revolution of the politically correct, that we can better understand what is at stake in the sexual revolution. At the same time, we all should recognize its effects: the tragedy of harm in millions of lives, which I describe in this book. In two concluding chapters, I offer some strategies that can help turn around the prevalent sexual decadence of our times and offer healing to its victims.

Many people would angrily reject my claim that the sexual revolution has any "victims", or that it has caused a "tragedy of harm in millions of lives". They see the revolution differently. For them it is a great advance in progress, freedom, human rights, and the individual's quest for happiness. I invite them to pause and look more closely at the story of this complex social and political movement which, while it may have benefitted some, has brought misery and oppression to many others.

They may also imagine that I do not respect the sincerity of those who have shaped and promoted various streams and causes in this revolution. I do not doubt the sincerity of social crusaders such as Margaret Sanger, nor do I question the scientific ideals of sexologists who analyze human sexual behavior. But sincerity is not enough. The misuse of religion demonstrates that principle. Nor are good intentions enough. The worst epitaph one could write on a tomb would be, "He meant well ..."

It is obvious that the United States has played a major role in the development of the sexual revolution, particularly in popularizing it. We need only think of Margaret Sanger, Alfred Kinsey, Masters and Johnson, Margaret Mead, Hugh Hefner, Allen Ginsberg, Saul Alinsky, gay liberation and LGBTQ, abortion as a "choice", gender feminism, the pornography industry, the decadent side of Hollywood, and the social media of our times. Ideologues developed ideas from Europe and the United Kingdom and popularized them in a U.S. context. They fueled an international political movement working for legislation in favor of sexual permissiveness.

Marriage and the family bear the brunt of the sexual revolution, and the young are a specific target. That explains how this book began—as lectures that I gave at the John Paul II Institute for Marriage and Family, Melbourne, of which I was director from 2004 to 2019. The lectures comprised part of a course to train teachers to assist parents to form children and young people with a good education in human sexuality, which is not only the parents' right, but their *duty*, particularly in these times.

The late Prof. Nicholas Tonti-Filippini together with his wife, Dr. Mary Walsh, planned and provided the course, and I am grateful for their work. I thank Dr. Ron and Mavis Pirola for their insights into a nuptial understanding of the goodness of human sexuality, and Pat Byrne for sharing his invaluable research into gender theory and ideology, published as *Transgender, One Shade of Grey*. I thank my cousin, Dr. Patricia Rooke, for reviewing the ideological history. I also thank Fr. John Flader and Fr. Jim Tierney for highlighting the role of the 2007 *Yogyakarta Principles* that promote the sexual revolution and for technical data on the difference between the two sexes.

The rise of the sexual revolution has also revealed that many people know little or nothing about what the Church teaches on marriage, sexuality, and the family. Therefore, as a guide to the wisdom the Church offers, I have added two appendices: 1. *Where to Find Catholic Teaching on Human Sexuality* and 2. *Where to Find Catholic Teaching on Education in Human Sexuality*.

The Holy Spirit moves freely through the wreckage of our fallen humanity. Our loving and patient God can bring good out of sin, disorder, and chaos. Christians, Jews, and men and women of goodwill should recognize the signs of hope and the prospect of rebuilding the virtues and values of what Saint John Paul II called the "*Civilization of Love*".

I obviously work from a Catholic perspective, but I seek to reach out to other Christians and especially to our spiritual forebears, the Jews. We are all in this struggle. This is an ecumenical project of people of faith, rejecting and reversing the ruthless actions of legislatures and tribunals that enforce the sexual revolution in various nations.

Some disturbing questions arise. How does the sexual revolution fit into a wider social revolution, driven by fashionable "woke" celebrities, wealthy individuals, and interest groups? Is that revolution exploiting homosexuals and transsexuals to further its power goals? Worst of all, is the pedophile agenda emerging again?

At the same time, in the great "field hospital" of the Church, we are called to work with compassion for the healing of many women, men, and children whose lives have been damaged, even ruined, by the sexual revolution. This book does not pass judgment on them. They are the victims. They need mercy, healing, and hope.

Most Rev. Peter J. Elliott
Melbourne, 2022

I

The Revolution Begins

ONLY HISTORY CAN GIVE US an understanding of the "sexual revolution" of our times. This "revolution" did not come from nowhere, nor did it suddenly burst into life in the mid-twentieth century. It took several centuries to build up, and at first it emerged gradually. This is why some may wonder whether "revolution" accurately describes a series of accelerating waves of permissiveness, especially when we go back into the past and examine the patterns and factors that have led us to where we are now.

The social history of human sexual behavior reveals major trends that are rather predictable, for example:

- There are *cycles* when public morality changes, marked by a "swing" from a puritanical to a permissive age or vice versa.
- Some people maintain marital fidelity while others misbehave sexually no matter what the current fashion may be.
- Other people are prone to the influence of the dominant trend of the age, usually set by influential people or "role models", today through the media and "celebrities".
- Permissiveness flourishes especially at the social extremes—amid wealth or poverty.

- In every society, there are some hedonists—pleasure-seeking men and women who believe the purpose of life is just "to have a good time".
- Prostitution is found in all societies.
- Illegitimate births are common in many societies.
- Pedophilia afflicts all societies.

Turning to the science of cultural anthropology, we find that in traditional societies permissive sexual behavior is tolerated more among males than among females. There are exceptions, such as in the Trobriand Islands and among the Wodaabe nomads in Africa, yet even here female permissive behavior is governed by specific social rules. However, in this book, the primary focus is Europe, which was the cradle of the sexual revolution as it affects us today.

Trends and Swings

In the seventeenth century, in post-Reformation Europe, we enter a world where sexual morality was based on marriage, derived from the Judeo-Christian ethical tradition, and grounded in the Bible and Church teachings. That is not to say that Christian societies, whether Catholic or Protestant, were perfect models of morality. But in this era we first find a significant swing toward stricter sexual morality.

Religious reform movements effect changes in society by shaping the way people live their daily lives. In the sixteenth century, Calvinism and similar severe forms of Protestantism produced the Puritans in England, Scotland, and the American colonies. In the seventeenth century within the Catholic Church, the Jansenists played a similar moralistic role, particularly in the Low Countries and

France. However, later in the seventeenth century, in both England and France, a liberalizing reaction set in, focused around the Crown. This was a time when the life-styles of powerful monarchs set social fashions.

In 1660, after the death of the Puritan dictator Oliver Cromwell, the Restoration of King Charles II and the example of his own life-style led to some loosening of private morality. In France, the "Sun King", Louis XIV, and his mistresses set a permissive tone, until he married a commoner, Madame de Maintenon, who ensured that her Jesuit friends converted him to better ways. His immediate successor, Louis XV, was openly promiscuous, and once more permissiveness characterized the higher levels of society, centered around the Court of Versailles.

At least among the wealthy nobility, eighteenth-century Europe saw a swing toward permissiveness, evident in the spread of printed pornography and the fashion of taking a mistress or lover. At this time, something more significant was also shaping sexual morality.

The Trigger of the Enlightenment

A new rational attitude to the sexual behavior of men and women was promoted in the name of *the Enlightenment* and a scientific understanding of human beings and society. That radical strand in the Enlightenment was the trigger of the sexual revolution.

The skeptics Voltaire (1694–1778), David Hume (1711–1776), and Jean-Jacques Rousseau (1712–1778) viewed human beings as basically rational "living machines", not morally responsible to a Creator God—if, indeed, such a God exists. Their disciples saw sexual freedom as helping to liberate men and women from the bondage of religious traditions and superstitions, which they blamed on Christian civilization. Literate people were encouraged to question accepted customs and conventions, even the ties of marriage and the family.

At the same time, taken as a whole, the Enlightenment was not permissive. While religious traditions were questioned during the Enlightenment, inherited Christian moral principles were applied to social and political issues. Drawing on the principles of Natural Law, the Founding Fathers of the United States sought to shape a new nation "under God" that protected every human being's right to "life, liberty, and the pursuit of happiness". Conventional respect for family and property was maintained. This is where the American Revolution differed from the French Revolution and the anti-Christian direction it took.

The new morality of the radical strand in the Enlightenment spread by way of the *French Revolution*. Anti-Christian revolutionary ideology attacked traditional Christian morality, with repercussions well beyond France. Novel social legislation reflected the change. *Civil marriages and divorce* were introduced, first under the Jacobins during the radical phase of the Revolution, then under **Napoleon Bonaparte** (1769–1821) in his Code. This change in civil law weakened the social influence of Catholic teaching on indissolubility and fidelity in marriage. As a French actress remarked at the time of change, "A Republican marriage is the sacrament of adultery."

Protestant societies were already vulnerable to these changes due to the weaker Lutheran and Calvinist interpretations of the indissolubility of marriage. While the post-Napoleonic era was marked by some positive reactions, particularly through the Catholic Revival, secular marriage laws remained intact. People do not easily give up what has come to suit them.

Romanticism

In the early nineteenth century, much of a growing trend toward permissiveness nevertheless remained hidden. Some people chose to lead double lives, outwardly conforming to prevailing moral and religious conventions, but secretly living as "libertines", that is, as men and women liberated from sexual mores.

By contrast, still inspired by the extreme phase of the French Revolution, some political radicals adopted an openly libertine life-style. The emotive mood and fashion of Romanticism inspired various writers, poets, artists, and composers in Europe and Britain, who defied and derided religious and moral conventions. **Lord George Byron** (1788–1824) was an active bisexual who anticipated later trends. His atheist friends, the renowned poet **Percy Bysshe Shelley** (1792–1822) and his mistress and second wife **Mary Shelley** (1797–1851), were also involved in radical political circles.[1]

In France, Catholic moral conventions were rejected by influential figures in the literary world. Non-political Romanticism inspired the poet **Charles Baudelaire** (1821–1867), who defied morality and the categories of good and evil in his writings and life-style. Embracing Romanticism along with radical politics, the notable writer **George Sand** (Amantine Dupin, 1804–1876) was a liberated woman.

---

[1] Their complex sexual relationships are brought out in the 2018 film *Mary Shelley*, but she is best remembered as the author of *Frankenstein*, a myth that suggests the collapse of a biblical understanding of human nature.

Her life was marked by a series of affairs, including a sad relationship with the Polish composer Chopin.

Key Influences

In Britain, the nearly sixty-four-year reign of Queen Victoria (1838–1901) was characterized by a swing toward sexual propriety and modesty, influenced by the Anglican queen herself and her Lutheran husband, Prince Albert (1819–1861). They set a widely admired example for stable family life, based on their married love. However, four British thinkers were already paving the way for a permissiveness that would respect neither marriage nor the family.

Jeremy Bentham (1748–1832) proposed his influential philosophy of *utilitarianism*—seeking the greatest happiness for the greatest number. But optimizing happiness in terms of pleasure (hedonism) can become an egotistical quest for gratification with obvious effects in the area of sexual behavior. This pragmatic atheist exercised great influence over legal theory, and, significantly, he undermined the Natural Law tradition in Britain by favoring a breach between ethics and law. To put this simply: what is legal need not necessarily be morally right.

Bentham's contemporary Rev. Thomas Malthus (1766–1834), a country vicar and economist, was an unwitting accomplice in the slide toward permissiveness. His theory of the threat of overpopulation obviously called for remedies. To reduce the birth rate, he proposed "moral restraint", meaning continence before marriage and late marriages. But Malthus was interpreted by his disciples, known as *neo-Malthusians*, to justify controlling births by artificial means, principally the use of the primitive condom and *coitus interruptus*.

Another powerful factor emerged in the early nineteenth century—*eugenics*. The neo-Malthusian scientist Francis Galton (1822–1911) promoted what he called *eugenics*, meaning the planned breeding of human beings in order to improve the quality of the human race.

Eugenics takes three forms:

- *Social eugenics* aims at reducing the numbers of the poor.
- *Health eugenics* is directed toward eliminating hereditary diseases and inherited disabilities, mental or physical.
- *Racial eugenics* aims at reducing the numbers of certain races, deemed to be "inferior" or "undesirable".

John Stuart Mill (1806–1873), a British philosopher and economist, was strongly influenced by Bentham. Like his father, James Mill, he was a keen neo-Malthusian. His radical understanding of freedom greatly contributed to the development of *liberalism*. His doctrine of permitting all actions that do not "affect prejudicially the interests of others" was the basis of the principle of "privacy", later to be invoked in favor of "pro-choice" on abortion and "free consent" for private sexual acts and the self-centered concept of human "autonomy".

Charles Darwin (1809–1882) raised basic questions about human behavior with his theory of evolution. His description of natural selection was influenced by early eugenicists. In turn, he influenced other eugenicists, such as his cousin, Francis Galton. But there are moral implications once men and women begin to regard themselves as "descended from apes" (a simplistic version of his theory). They begin to question what really constitutes "right and wrong".

Evolutionary theory has ethical implications:

- Can it be argued that morality also evolved and is still evolving, hence open to change?
- Can it also be argued that a superior species could create its own "higher morality", perhaps breaking the conventions and taboos of earlier phases of biological and social evolution?
- Can it even be argued that sex is an animal instinct with laws of its own, not necessarily tied to social conventions or religious moral principles?

But who was willing or daring enough to put social Darwinian theories into practice? Here we turn to the emergence of the major ideological streams of radical socialism.

The Ideology of the Left

Radical nineteenth-century political movements, such as anarchism, included agendas for "free love" and "open marriage", that is, a marriage where both parties remain free to have sexual relations with others outside their marriage. This permissiveness was implicit in the atheistic redefinition of the human person, for example as "economic man", according to **Karl Marx** (1818–1883).

In a Marxist perspective, men and women are no longer responsible to a Creator God but are the products of blind evolutionary forces, subject to the inevitable social and economic laws of history. Yet once equipped with class-consciousness and engaging in the class war, the human person is the maker of his destiny. The goal is *utopia*, heaven on earth, a socialist paradise. But that can be attained only through revolutions to bring down the capitalist class and to destroy its system.

Marriage, family, and religion are easily identified as oppressive elements of the conventional bourgeois society that must be overthrown by the working class, the proletariat. This political movement became known as *Communism*. In the twentieth century, *Marxism* would mutate and become a potent vector of the sexual revolution.

The Time of Transition

Less extreme political and social movements converged, largely under the banner of liberalism. Society in Europe and North America had left behind both the old order of Christendom and the age of absolute monarchs and had entered an era of imperialism and free enterprise, with economic growth and wider prosperity based on industry and colonies. Most societies were becoming more democratic, at least for males with money. Nationalism and competitive trade would lead to World War I (1914–1918). The separation between religion and society, church and state, was clearer, a trend we now call *secularization*. This was a fertile field for some of the changes that would mark the open appearance of the sexual revolution. A mood of toleration, pluralism, and freedom of opinion and life-style was spreading.

Romanticism continued to inspire others to break social conventions in the way they lived. The much-admired actress Sarah Bernhardt (1844–1923) inherited the profession of her mother, a *courtesan*, that is, a high-class prostitute whose clients were rich and powerful men. Courtesans were tolerated in France, with role models going back to the royal mistresses of the seventeenth century. In this atmosphere, we find the romantic illusion that "love" means sexual union.

In the last decades of the nineteenth century, a romantic *cult of beauty* also promoted sensuous themes, breaking down moral conventions through innovative literature, poetry, and art. English "aesthetes" such as Oscar Wilde (1854–1900), Ronald Firbank (1886–1926), and Aubrey Beardsley (1872–1898), and the French "decadents", Arthur Rimbaud (1854–1891), Paul Verlaine (1844–1896), and André Gide (1869–1951), anticipated the emergence from the shadows of the hidden homosexual subculture, outraging yet fascinating the public. Most of these gifted but flawed men died as penitent Catholics. But they had opened doors, and they set fashions of behavior among the young.

An early champion of homosexuality, Edward Carpenter (1844–1929), influenced the notable writer E. M. Forster (1879–1970). In the wider sense of defending sensuality, he also influenced D. H. Lawrence (1885–1930), whose novel *Lady Chatterley's Lover* would later become a major issue in the British movement to end censorship.

At this stage, reactions against nineteenth-century faith in science and rationalism took the form of occultism and neo-paganism, for example, in "theosophy", a religious cocktail that would later influence the "New Age" movement. Occultists invested sexual permissiveness with mystical significance, some even sliding into the sexual variations of Satanism.

By the end of the nineteenth century, as these trends converged, we perceive a transition to more open and tolerated permissiveness. In England, the "Gay Nineties" and the post-Victorian era of King Edward VII (1841–1910), who kept mistresses, saw a reaction against conventions, one of those "swings" in public morality. In English literature and theater, H. G. Wells (1866–1946), George Bernard Shaw (1856–1950), and the "Bohemian" Fabians represented the breakdown of conventional morality. The

Fabian socialists were an atheistic intellectual elite based in London, influencing the middle classes through their socialist proposals and widely read books.

"Prophets" of the Sexual Revolution

The late-nineteenth-century transition also moved on other more stable levels that would have lasting effects. Influential thinkers and activists now separated sexual behavior not only from objective morality but, more significantly, from having children.

Sigmund Freud (1856–1939) tried to penetrate human behavior through psychoanalysis. For Freud, sexuality was the dominating instinct, the driving power of the *libido*, which Christians tend to equate, not always accurately, with concupiscence. In spite of this *pansexualism*, which is a part of his theory, Freud was not in favor of allowing the libido to dominate a person. However, he provided the scientific justification for moving away from sexuality directed toward procreation to sexuality directed toward pleasure because he emphasized sex as the driving instinct that had to be confronted, understood, and accepted.

The Sexologists

The observation and analysis of human sexual behavior emerged in central Europe as the science of *sexology*, pioneered by the German psychiatrist Richard von Krafft-Ebing (1840–1902), whose *Psychopathia Sexualis* first appeared in 1886. In 1906, the German psychiatrist Iwan Bloch (1872–1922) published *The Sexual Life of Our Time in Its Relations to Modern Civilization*. In this work, the nineteenth-century scientific mentality is applied using observation and a descriptive method for the study of all forms of human sexual behavior. Krafft-Ebing and Bloch respected moral values and modesty, but their descriptive method already marks a shift from understanding sexuality in terms of morality and human relationships to regarding sexuality as *morally neutral animal behavior* that can be described, analyzed, and classified. In this era, the categories *heterosexual, homosexual,* and *bisexual* first came to be used.

Havelock Ellis (1859–1939), a British physician, psychologist, and essayist, published the first medical study of homosexuality in 1897. However, in his seven-volume work, *Studies in the Psychology of Sex*, sexology merged with psychology and produced a mystique of eroticism. This seemed more romantic and less rationalistic than analytical German sexology, but it was based on the pseudoscientific definition of the person as a rational animal whose drives and instincts must be satisfied through "free love". Ellis worked with the German sexologist and pioneer of homosexual activism, **Magnus Hirschfeld** (1868–1935), who had also collaborated with Bloch.

Nevertheless, the early research of European sexology should not be set aside lightly. Nor does it always endorse permissiveness. A former disciple of Freud, the psychologist **Wilhelm Stekel** (1868–1940), would not be politically correct today. Through case studies set out in *The Homosexual Neurosis* (1922), Stekel offered a moderate and plausible explanation for same-sex attraction, activity, and relationships. But his use of the word "neurosis" damns him in the eyes of modern ideologues whose use of sexology is selective.

What the sexologists achieved was a *new understanding of sex*. In the context of European liberalism and demands for human freedom, they focused on the individual and his *inner residing sexuality*. Sex thus moves beyond biology, reproduction, procreation, and the boundaries and restraints of social convention and morality. The sexologists affirmed the sexual identity of the individual, in his mind, his emotions, desires, drives, and complexes. This is the power engine for the sexual revolution. In effect, it moves sex from the body to the mind.

Powerful Women

So far, the dominant influences have been men. Now women begin to enter the field. The feminism of this era was mainly a struggle for female suffrage and equal marriage and property rights. Only on the extreme wing of nineteenth- and early twentieth-century feminism do we find the "new woman" practicing "free love", which was rejected by many of the suffragettes, who also opposed abortion and birth control.

However, something more destructive appeared in the United States. Margaret Sanger (1879–1966) was a wealthy New York Leftist who had been a disciple and, for a time, the mistress of Havelock Ellis. Her married life included various sexual adventures. But her public focus was on controlling fertility. Beginning in 1915, she resolutely worked to promote contraception among all women and even went to prison for her cause. She was motivated by concern to reduce pregnancies among poor women and a sincere effort to free them from the "fear of pregnancy" and the "burden of childbearing". She wanted to reduce the numbers of the poor and used the slogan *"More children from the fit: less from the unfit; that is the chief aim of birth control"*. No one need doubt that her social conscience and the women's issues she sought to resolve were real. She was guided by feminism, sexology, and those recurring myths: the danger of overpopulation and especially the need to breed a purer, healthier human race—neo-Malthusian eugenics. But her commitment to eugenics led her to racist opinions that would take a deadly political form.

The forces that converged in Sanger's work would all play a role in the sexual revolution of the final decades of the twentieth century:

- Leftist ideology,
- free love,
- birth control,
- neo-Malthusian eugenics,
- sexology,
- Freudian analysis,
- value-free sex education,
- radical feminism,
- easy divorce,
- occultism,
- drugs.

In England, **Marie Stopes** (1880–1958) zealously proclaimed the gospel of birth control. Thanks to her family background, she was devoted to eugenics. In 1913, this skilled scientist and sincere campaigner met up with Margaret Sanger. In 1918, she published *Married Love*, a controversial manual promoting contraception in marriage. At least in public, Marie Stopes strongly opposed abortion. Yet abortion "clinics" are named after her today, operating under the banner of *Marie Stopes International*.

Similar crusading figures were active in Europe, working to change restrictive laws on birth control and abortion and seeking to influence the medical profession. But at a global level, Margaret Sanger would prove to be the most effective pioneer of the sexual revolution.

2

The Revolution Emerges

WORLD WAR I (1914–1918) separated millions of men from their wives for years and forced most of them to live under terrible conditions, such as prevailed during trench warfare. The vast conflict threw citizens from various nations and all social levels into situations they would never have experienced at home. The horrors of the war and the deep inner wounds of survivors led to a questioning of traditional values. Some found deeper religious faith, but others slid into despair, skepticism, confusion, or an escapist quest for pleasure. Such conflicting views of life were what the soldiers brought home with them together with their wounds in body and mind.

The era after the war saw another swing, a further loosening of sexual morality, the "Roaring Twenties". While some Europeans were influenced by permissive "cabaret" life-styles in Paris and Berlin, the United States was increasingly guided by Hollywood and a glamorous romantic sexuality expressed in films and popular music. The permissiveness of a prosperous minority was loosening morals among the masses. The role models were actors, the first generation of what would later be known as "celebrities". While we should not exaggerate this influence, because many people remained insulated from it, the emerging permissive attitudes were able to spread widely through increased literacy, the developing mass media, and easier travel.

At this stage, we see a gradual acceptance of two key factors that would drive the sexual revolution, namely, easier access to:

- *divorce*, facilitating the breakdown of stable relationships;
- *contraceptive birth control*, a rejection of the fertile dimension of sex.

The stigma of divorce was erased by the view that marriage is a convenient legal arrangement, "only a piece of paper". Hollywood publicized actors who divorced and remarried, and stories of their infidelities abounded in the entertainment media. Yet in the era of the Depression, the sex symbols became celebrities, glamorous creations of the media, even a tragic figure like **Jean Harlow** (1911–1937), who died at the height of her career, or the comedienne **Mae West** (1893–1980), who specialized in double entendres when sound came to the screen.

However, birth control would emerge as a more significant social factor than Hollywood role models. Margaret Sanger was active in the 1920s and '30s, preaching contraceptive birth control and blending her belief in eugenics with popular racism, even of a Nazi hue.

In 1930, the first Christian bastion against contraceptive birth control was breached when the Anglican bishops at the Lambeth Conference tacitly approved the use of contraceptives. The rapid response of **Pope Pius XI** (1857–1939) in the encyclical *Casti connubii* firmly upheld Catholic teaching against contraception in the context of clearer teaching on sacramental marriage.

In terms of sexual morality, these contrasting events show not only how far people had moved in their attitudes, but also what the key to a full-blown sexual revolution would be—*the separation of procreation from sexual intercourse.* What was implied by philosophers and sexologists was put into practice by Sanger and her allies. The way to sexual liberation was to *sterilize sexual activity*, eliminating fertility and freeing sex from childbearing. Sex is now understood as residing in the mind, in emotions, impulses, and drives.

Pope Pius XI also recognized the threat of permissive projects to form the young. This explains his denunciation of *sex education* in 1929, in the encyclical *Divini illius magistri*. Already, within some State systems of education, naturalist sex education was being provided to promote "health" and sexual freedom among the young. This is also called "value-free sex education" to distinguish it from a prudent education in human sexuality shaped by Christian ethics, which the pope encouraged.

If permissive views were spreading, the full effects were yet to be felt. The era of the economic Depression of the 1930s also saw some sobering-up in Hollywood, with tighter censorship of films under the Hays Code, the Motion Picture Production Code (1930). This ran parallel with the final years of the prohibition of alcohol in the United States.

However, the *divorce mentality*, cultivated by role models from Hollywood, was clearly gaining ground. In 1936, King Edward VIII (1894–1972) abdicated the throne of England because he was not permitted to marry Wallis Simpson (1896–1986), a twice-married divorcée, but public opinion supported him. Through laws steadily leading to no-fault divorce, the State would prove to be decisive in that field.

Four lay Christian thinkers and writers, in varying degrees, perceived deteriorating sexual trends in the collapse of morals that developed during the interwar era:

G.K. Chesterton (1874–1936), C.S. Lewis (1898–1963), and especially Christopher Dawson (1889–1970) and Dietrich von Hildebrand (1889–1977). They all witnessed the fading of a European culture based on religion and the family. In 1926, Chesterton predicted the current sexual revolution.[1]

In this era, the rise of secularism and the modern authoritarian State provided the context for the permissiveness that would expand in the later decades of the twentieth century. This was the age of the centralized State systems led by dictators, the making of a new kind of society, a new social order where the State exercises total control over every detail of our lives—*totalitarianism.*

The Totalitarians

Whether on the Left or the Right, the totalitarian systems represented a double standard in sexual morality. For example, Italian Fascism supported public morality and law and order, but while Benito Mussolini (1883–1945) was depicted as a "family man", he was promiscuous. The men who held power in the totalitarian systems felt free to live as they pleased, no matter what the government policy was on morality.

1. Sexual Morality in the Third Reich

After he took power in Germany in 1933, Adolf Hitler (1889–1945) ostensibly purged the homosexuals from the Nazi Party to justify his move against Ernst Röhm, leader

---

[1] G.K. Chesterton, in *The Catholic Church and Conversion* (1926; San Francisco: Ignatius Press, 2006), in the final chapter, predicts a split in the Church over sexual morality; and he wrote forty-two years before *Humanae vitae.*

of the Brownshirts, a revolutionary army of National Socialism. But the supposed Northern European taste for same-sex activity remained intact. Among the elite guard of the Nazi Reich known as the S.S., macho homosexual activity was condoned.[2] At the same time, other homosexuals were sent to concentration camps, forced to wear an inverted pink triangle, ensuring maltreatment, torture, and even death. Such moral duplicity in the Third Reich still arouses controversy.

Among the Nazis, we find the abiding influence of Friedrich Nietzsche (1844–1900) and his ideal Darwinian "superman" who has risen above conventional morality.[3] Nazis linked this ideal of the superman to achieving racial purity through eugenics. Therefore, like stallions on a stud farm, the S.S. officers could father Aryan children, while at the same time the Reich propaganda ministry extolled Germanic family values: motherhood, childbearing, and housekeeping. The German wife and mother was an idealized figure, but the Party chiefs kept mistresses. To promote Nazi racist eugenics, Aryans were forbidden to have abortions, but Slavs were encouraged to abort their children. During the Second World War, the Nazi State took eugenics to its most ruthless level by systematically eliminating the "unfit" and the "useless eaters". Thousands of men, women, and children in institutions for people with mental or physical disabilities were murdered. Opposed and halted by the Catholic

---

[2] As argued by Scott Lively and Kevin Abrams in *The Pink Swastika: Homosexuality in the Nazi Party* (Sacramento, Calif.: Veritas Aeterna Press, 1995). This contested book contradicts revisionist views that assert a holocaust of homosexuals took place that was equivalent to the holocaust suffered by the Jews.

[3] Those promoting Nietzsche in universities today reject linking him with the Third Reich. He was not anti-Semitic, but his heroic super-male does fit the Fascist militarist and racial ideal.

Church, the Nazi *T4 euthanasia program* nevertheless continued secretly until the end of the war. It is here that we find a mysterious link between sex and death. *Loss of respect for sexual morality and decency is intertwined with a loss of respect for human life.*

2. Sexual Morality in Soviet Communism

After the Russian Revolution in 1917, Soviet Communism at first reflected a more complex yet ultimately enduring collapse of sexual morality. This was based on the materialistic Marxist redefinition of the person as the subject of the inevitable economic forces of history. After the Revolution, the Leninist "utopian" phase was influenced by radical prerevolutionary ideas, including feminism. Access to a no-fault divorce was made easy, and marriage was reduced to "just a piece of paper". Abortion was permitted.

From Vladimir Lenin (1870–1924) and Leon Trotsky (1879–1940) came the Communist strategy of "entryism", that is, the penetration of existing political groups or organizations, which are then taken over and used for revolutionary purposes. At the same time, Lenin perceived the need to undermine and weaken conventional Judeo-Christian morality in the West as part of the Communists' international strategy to pave the way for world revolution. Combined with entryism, this strategy was taken up in a Freudian pansexual direction by some breakaway Marxists who formed the Frankfurt School, which I will examine later in the context of the wider social revolution of our times.

In the era of the dictator Joseph Stalin (1878–1953), the Leninist permissive tendency was reversed. Marriage was strengthened, abortion was restricted. The Russian family and even religion were enlisted in Stalin's massive war effort to defeat Nazi Germany. Stalin himself was promiscuous. And, after he died, there was some loosening-up, at least in restoring easy access to abortion, which became a method of birth control.

What remains constant throughout the Communist swings of morality is *expediency*. What is deemed moral or immoral, right or wrong, is whatever suits the practical policies of the Party at a particular time—based on the atheistic denial that there is any objective morality. This accounts for the collapse of family stability in former Communist countries, a tragic inheritance lingering to this day.

The Critical Postwar Era

World War II had similar liberalizing effects to World War I. One factor was the widespread use of the condom by soldiers as a prophylactic against venereal disease. The men may not have brought disease home to their wives, but some did bring back contraceptive birth control or habitual recourse to prostitutes. However, on the surface, this second postwar era seemed more sober. Was it not marked by a "baby boom", an emphasis on rebuilding nations through marriage and children? At the same time, other forces were at work, and it is not true to characterize the 1950s as an age of conservatism or "sexual repression". This was the critical era when the sexual revolution emerged into the public forum.

Having carefully set aside their racist flirtations with the defeated Nazis, the neo-Malthusians were soon back in action, working to exert global influence in the postwar era of the United Nations. In 1952, Margaret Sanger crowned her disordered life by founding the *International*

Planned Parenthood Federation, her greatest and most lasting achievement, today the world's largest provider and promoter of abortion and birth control. But the "day" of IPPF was still to come.

Radical pansexualism flourished among some intellectuals. In addition to Freud, we find new influences, and they are atheists. The French existentialist **Jean-Paul Sartre** (1905–1980) argued that, if there is no God, then everything is permitted and morality is whatever the individual wills. In *The Second Sex* (1949), his mistress, **Simone de Beauvoir** (1908–1986), described the male-female relationship as oppression by males and called for the liberation of women from childbearing, which she detested. De Beauvoir was thus a guiding influence in developing modern feminism. She reworked the Marxist class war into a war between the sexes: males oppressing females who need to be liberated.

Another influence in the English-speaking world was British analytic philosophy, which went beyond Bentham and Mill by way of logic and language theory. Morality was seen as only words, value-laden language that is fundamentally meaningless. Each person is free to construct his own value system, as did the mathematician and philosopher **Bertrand Russell** (1872–1970), one of the founders of analytic philosophy. His long life of political activism was marked by four marriages and various affairs. Once again, we see how an articulate and respected atheist is able to influence social trends in the name of a secular humanism. But, analytical philosophy is not necessarily atheistic or morally permissive.[4]

---

[4] For example, Elizabeth Anscombe, a notable English analytic philosopher, was a devout Catholic, radically pro-life, and a champion of the encyclical *Humanae vitae*, as I can attest from having known her.

Influenced by feminism and schemes for social engineering, the European democratic Left favored permissive sexual morality. The social democratic societies of Scandinavia became laboratories for systematic sex education and for greater sexual freedom among the young, especially women.

Much popular literature in the 1950s was characterized by sexual permissiveness. Although censorship restricted the circulation of explicit pornography, glossy "soft porn" was gradually appearing. The magazine *Playboy* was founded in 1953. Another loosening-up of morals emerged in Hollywood. The "sex goddesses" of the 1950s, such as **Marilyn Monroe** (1926–1962) and **Jayne Mansfield** (1933–1967), represented a more explicit sexuality than the early Hollywood "vamp". An amoral actress became a "celebrity" whose life was a model for permissive behavior. Once-forbidden themes began to appear in books and on the silver screen, for example, under-age sex in *Lolita*. In the early 1960s, an improbable film character, James Bond (British Agent 007), had "a license to kill" and to have liaisons with whatever woman he desired.

The *science of sexology* took a leap forward using the fashionable behaviorist method. An American scientist, **Alfred Kinsey** (1894–1956), published what are known as the Kinsey Reports, that is, *Sexual Behavior in the Human Male* (1948) and *Sexual Behavior in the Human Female* (1953). Funded by the Rockefeller Foundation, his research on 12,000 humans was based on observation and inquiry. The *Reports* are still cited, notwithstanding allegations that later emerged: that sex offenders were used for research purposes and that children were molested. Kinsey concluded that nothing sexual is "normal" or "abnormal", nothing sexual is "right" or "wrong". The high Kinsey statistic still cited for male homosexuals ("one in ten men") was later criticized as an exaggeration, but in the twenty-first century, this statistic would become a standard propaganda slogan from the LGBTQ lobby.

In the field of cultural anthropology, **Margaret Mead** (1901–1978) became a proponent of sexual freedom, based on her research on the habits of young people growing up in Samoa. Years later, her research was found to rest largely on mischievous lies invented by the Samoans to make a fool of the foreigner. But her discredited work was cited to justify the myth of a "paradise" based on sexual liberation, which we can also trace back to Rousseau's ideal of the "noble savage" and a denial of Original Sin.

3

On Three Shaky Foundations

B Y THE MID-1960S, a revolution in sexual morality was visible and vocal, and the media and entertainment industry eagerly took it up. Before we consider these trends, it is important to understand that radical changes in sexual morality and behavior were based on three foundations:

1. *the rejection of God, at least a God who is involved in our lives;*
2. *a radical change in understanding the nature of the human person;*
3. *separating human sexuality from fertility.*

Foundation 1. *The rejection of God*

Atheism usually takes two forms:

1. *formal or philosophical atheism*, which is defended rationally by people like Richard Dawkins (1941–), and
2. *practical atheism*, which tends to be irrational, more a feeling, lacking in arguments and prone to justify itself by mocking religion.

Today, practical atheism is more widespread. People live and act *as if there were no God*. But they are really rejecting a God who is interested in human moral behavior, that is, the God who gave us the Ten Commandments, including "You shall not commit adultery." This God created us with a natural moral sense, the Natural Law, by implanting a conscience in each of us. But for some people, this God is very inconvenient, a burden, a cause of guilt, etc., who must be brushed aside because this interfering God "cramps my style".

Practical atheists are often materialists. For them, the only reality is matter—what we can see, touch, measure, and weigh. Therefore, life revolves around practical realities, particularly finance, buying and selling, getting and keeping things. "Materialism", in the popular meaning of the word, means being attached to things such as money, property, fashion, and "having a good time". This often takes the form of consumerism, an obsessive interest in acquiring things, usually in obedience to advertising.

In the materialistic world of practical atheism, sex easily becomes a commodity. In the affluent societies, sex is "something" to get when you can, or a business, a game, a sport, play, recreation, part of having a good time. But then the human question arises, because this involves using people, turning a woman or a man into a "sexual object", a commodity, a thing rather than a person.

When we turn to the philosophical atheists, we find that they are materialists in a more sophisticated way, believing that the only reality is matter. I have named various intellectuals who pioneered the sexual revolution, and most of these men and women were atheists. Many of them identified themselves as *humanists*, promoters of a world view built, not around God, but around the human person, with ideals of freedom and creativity. However, they were not necessarily involved in the permissive currents of the sexual revolution.

Today, their ideological heirs may describe themselves as *humanists*, *secular humanists*, or *secularists*. However, we need to appreciate a change in the meaning of "secular". From simply referring to the "things of this world", since the mid-nineteenth century the term "secular" has come to refer to what is real and material as opposed to religious beliefs. Secularists claim that theirs is a scientific world view. In reality, the basis is a nineteenth-century understanding of science that is materialist and godless.

When applied to society, this mentality is expressed in "the secular state", which goes beyond the American dogma of "The separation of church and state" to the goal of the *total secularization of society*. By describing themselves as "humanists", these atheists still lay claim to ethical principles of justice and human rights, and I do not doubt their sincerity. Yet their world view has easily succumbed to the ideologies and destructive projects outlined in this book.

Today, permissive influences often, not always, come from "the Left". The Marxist ideology of dialectical materialism is atheistic. It survived the fall of the Soviet Union because it had already mutated into what is called "cultural Marxism". However, some nonpolitical neo-atheists manage to combine rationality with a raging anger against all religion. This includes abusive criticism directed against conventional morality and "people of faith".

In his incisive encyclical letter *Fides et ratio* (1993), **Saint John Paul II** (1920–2005) indicated another rising force, "postmodernism". According to some currents of postmodern thought, "the time of certainties is irrevocably past, and the human being must now learn to live in a horizon of total absence of meaning, where everything is provisional and ephemeral ..." (FR, 91). We shall see how this loss of meaning guides genderism.

An observable social effect of all forms of atheism is the widespread mood of *indifferentism,* an attitude of "I couldn't care less." If there is no God or if "God is dead" (whatever that means), "so what?", and we can go ahead and do what we like. This may be a form of *nihilism,* the belief that nothing matters.

The wise American social analyst **Fr. Richard Neuhaus** (1936–2009) put it this way: "*If bad things don't matter, then good things don't matter, and then nothing matters.*"[1] Or as Sartre (following Dostoyevsky) speculated, *if there is no God, then everything is permitted.*[2]

Foundation 2. *A radical change in understanding the nature of the human person*

What are we? What am I? Who am I? Why am I here? Where am I going?

Atheism offers unsatisfactory answers to these questions. Indeed, atheism can easily become a clever distraction, arguing on and on about God while not confronting the real issue, who we are and why we are here, leading into the broad ethical question: *How then are we to live?*

Both liberal individualists and Marxist collectivists regard men and women as clever animals, without a soul, without objective morality to guide them, without even a fixed nature. For its continuing growth, the sexual revolution depends on this materialist understanding of the human being, which is known as *naturalist anthropology.*

---

[1] Richard John Neuhaus, *Death on a Friday Afternoon: Meditations on the Last Words of Jesus from the Cross* (New York: Basic Books, 2001), p. 11.

[2] Jean-Paul Sartre, *Existentialism and Humanism,* trans. Philip Mairet (Eyre Methuen, 1973), pp. 33–34.

Autonomy

As already indicated, the materialist can easily use people as things, so that a woman or a man may become a "sexual object" rather than a person. This tendency is now reinforced by the politically correct concept of "autonomy", the *total independence of each human being*. Autonomy should be distinguished from "individualism", which *may* describe a healthy and creative human trait. Autonomy distorts the self-awareness of the individual, who becomes the "imperial self": *I alone* will choose. *I alone* will decide.

When we reflect on what "alone" means, the demand for autonomy breaks apart society, splits marriage and the family, and also undermines friendship and cooperation among people. Autonomy denies what scientific study and common sense endorse, that the human being is a "social animal". We all need one another. We depend on one another. No one is an island.

Beginning in our ancestral tribes, civilizations emerged and developed through this need for social interaction and cooperation, for relationships involving rights and duties, even ordered obligations and some sense of public service for "the common good". Marriage itself is the core example of the social nature of persons, to raise and protect young human beings, which is why the family is the basic living cell of all societies.

Dualism or the Body-Mind Problem

Autonomy also highlights something very strange that has intensified in the sexual revolution. From time to time across history, human beings have thought of themselves as living in two separate compartments at once, the body and the mind—or the body and the soul, for religious people.

The separation of body and mind is known as *dualism*. In modern Western thought, it goes back to René Descartes (1596–1650), a Catholic philosopher of immense influence who affirmed, "*I think, therefore I am.*"[3] He sharply separated the mind from the body and described the person as a spirit contained in a body. This concept was parodied by his critics as "the ghost in the machine".

Whatever they may have intended, the sexologists and Freudians moved in the direction of dualism. They focused on the individual and his *inner residing sexuality*. Sex is redefined, not in terms of biology, reproduction, or procreation, but as what is happening in the brain.

When we apply this dualist separation of mind from body to sexual behavior and morality, we come across the widespread opinion that *what we do with our bodies does not really matter, as long as the mind is pure*, in some sense. Madonna could sing about being "like a virgin" in her 1984 song, but who took her literally?

In a dualist perspective, my body becomes an instrument. It is not the "real me". The "real me" is my mind. Therefore, if I *mean* well, I can do what I like with my body. One caution is usually added—"as long as you do not harm anyone else", that is, until we get into some forms of sexual pleasure that involve pain. Then we are told that this is "all right—if they consent".

As we shall see, this dualism is activated in what I call *the war against the body*. You reject the biological reality of your body in gender theory, gender ideology, and transsexualism. So if you *identify* as the opposite sex in your mind, then that is what you become. After all, "it's all in the mind...."

---

[3] Descartes reversed what the Greco-Roman and Scholastic Catholic philosophies would affirm, "I am, therefore I think."

Dualism and *autonomy* work together. This partly explains the self-centered mentality of many of those who serve or succumb to the sexual revolution. They slide into a form of self-love or *narcissism* in which a mind is infatuated with its own body.

We see this happening all around us. Dualism and narcissism feed the troubling trend in our society of the *cult of the body*, an obsession with the "body beautiful", female or male. In some cases, this has a sexual dimension, particularly when an aging person tries to perpetuate youthfulness by projecting an image of sexual vigor or allure. By contrast, some young people seek a remodeling of their bodies because in a dualist mind-set, the body is like your clothing or an accessory you can put on or take off just as you wish.

Since the latter years of the twentieth century, surgical modification or "enhancement" of the body has become a major industry. The body becomes my main accessory to be adapted, shaped, and even given a "total makeover". Surgical, hormonal, and chemical projects are challenged only when they go wrong or produce bizarre effects with legal repercussions. It is no accident that body obsession reflects the current phase of the sexual revolution. Self-preoccupation is also associated with a fear of death and the accompanying pretense that death does not happen, because, as the song tells me, I am "forever young".

Foundation 3. *Separating sexuality from fertility*

In the mid-twentieth century, the third practical foundation made the sexual revolution possible: separating human sexuality from fertility; to put it simply, separating lovemaking from having children. It can be demonstrated that one tiny object made the current phase of the sexual revolution possible, a technological breakthrough: the *contraceptive pill*.[4]

We return to history. In 1953, Margaret Sanger obtained a large sum of money from a wealthy friend to finance the research of **Gregory Pincus** (1903–1967), co-inventor of an oral contraceptive, "the pill", which was launched in 1960. During the 1960s, the rapid spread of oral contraception eroded the "fear of pregnancy" and was hailed by feminists as the liberation of women from the burden of pregnancy and sexual constraints.

What had really happened was more subtle and devastating. Procreation had been separated from sex in a new way, hidden within a woman's body that had been rendered temporarily infertile. Now it was possible to regard sterile or infertile sexuality as the norm. Later, this separation would be completed in reverse—through new technologies of artificial procreation such as *in vitro fertilization*. But widespread contraception opened the door for something worse.

Abortion

In 1967, the "Mother of Parliaments" in Westminster legalized abortion. This legislation, hailed by feminists, was of great influence throughout the world, and the United States followed in 1973 with the U.S. Supreme Court *Roe versus Wade* ruling. This was a critical moment when the sexual revolution penetrated the State.[5]

---

[4] This is argued well by the founder of the Ruth Institute, Jennifer Roback Morse, in *The Sexual State: How Elite Ideologies Are Destroying Lives and Why the Church Was Right All Along* (Gastonia, N.C.: Tan Books, 2018).

[5] On June 24, 2022, in *Dobbs versus Jackson Women's Health Organization*, the U.S. Supreme Court upheld a state law restricting abortion. The decision overturned *Roe versus Wade* and returned to state legislators their authority to regulate abortion.

Abortion is essential to the sexual revolution. As contraception spread everywhere, it was obvious that there was no perfect method, so abortion became the remedy for contraceptive failure. As cohabitation and promiscuity spread, the legalized killing of the unborn became the neatest solution to the only sin that remained—the "unwanted" pregnancy. In 1965, the Second Vatican Council condemned abortion and infanticide as "abominable crimes" (*Gaudium et spes*, 55).

On July 25, 1968, after much reflection and consultation, **Pope Paul VI** (1897–1978) issued the encyclical letter *Humanae vitae*, the response of the Church to the anti-life manipulation of fertility and sexuality. With the authority of the successor of Saint Peter, he restated and sharpened Catholic teaching against abortion, contraception, and sterilization. He saw what was really involved in contraception— *separating life-giving from love-giving.* Saint Paul VI was also prophetic in his assertion that contraception would degrade and exploit women (cf. HV, 17). At the time, people ridiculed him for saying that. Today, some feminists make similar affirmations, although they never quote Saint Paul VI.

4

Revolution on the Streets:
The "Age of Aquarius"

THE SEXUAL REVOLUTION came out into the open in the
"Age of Aquarius" of the late 1960s and early 1970s.
Explicit musicals such as *Hair* and *Oh! Calcutta!* reflected
a wider cultural revolution, a reaction, so it was said, to
the staid ways of the dreary postwar years. Drugs, "psychedelic" pop culture, hippies shouting "*Make love, not
war*", the repetitive thump of rock music—these were the
sights and sounds of a revolutionary era, fueled by reaction
against the Vietnam War and continual radical propaganda
from the Left. The "swinging sixties" redefined adultery.
Adulterers now became "swingers" with "open marriages"
allowing sexual relations between "swinging couples".

In the era of the Woodstock youth festival and student
uprisings in the United States, activist **Saul Alinsky** (1909–
1972) promoted a social and cultural revolution along the
lines of cultural Marxism as articulated by **Herbert Marcuse** (1898–1979).

The Marxist existentialism of Marcuse, a German-
American philosopher, was popular among university
students and their teachers on the Paris Left Bank during
1968, the revolutionary year of student uprisings in various Western nations. He also brought the sexual opinions
of de Beauvoir and Sartre to a new generation of young

people. Marcuse identified sexual freedom with personal liberation from oppressive structures. He focused on homosexuals as an oppressed minority, a theme he had developed as early as 1955 in *Eros and Civilization*. If de Beauvoir reworked Marxism as liberation for women, so Marcuse reworked Marxism to free a sexual minority whose cause was taking shape as "gay liberation".

Inspired by Freud, Austrian medical doctor and psychoanalyst Wilhelm Reich (1897–1957) had already propounded this quasi-political approach. It was Reich who invented the expression "the sexual revolution", the title of his 1936 book. But Marcuse and Reich went beyond Freud in proclaiming the need for freedom from inhibitions. Freud maintained that restraints were needed to allow civilization to develop, for example, the taboo against incest, which protects the family. Marcuse promoted incest along with pedophilia.

Reich presented sexual liberation as a cleansing experience removing the guilt men and women are made to carry in a repressive bourgeois society. Marcuse went beyond Reich and saw the need for total liberation from *all* restraints in sexual behavior. Sexual license became a game with no distinctions between heterosexual and homosexual behavior, and a "polymorphous" sexuality became the ideal.

"Polymorphous" ("many forms", in Greek) describes a completely fluid, ever-changing sexuality, offering all variations and preferences. This ideal would later become a powerful feature of the *gender ideology* of the early twenty-first century. Marcuse attacked marriage and the family as oppression and bondage and rejected all moral limits to sexual expression required by them. In Marcuse, we find the anarchist strain on the radical side of Marxism. Marcuse was involved in the Frankfurt School, which is covered in chapter 6.

In the 1960s, sexology continued to be influenced by the Kinsey Reports, but this was soon overshadowed by the research of two Americans, **William H. Masters** (1915–2001) and **Virginia E. Johnson** (1925–2013). Their work included a development from closely observing behavior to therapy for sexual disorders, but without moral inhibitions. Their research was still set in a biological and behaviorist perspective and always focused on intercourse. Johnson abandoned her therapy program for homosexuals in 1977, after the American Psychiatric Association removed homosexuality from mental disorders (in 1973).

Economic changes in the 1960s and 1970s provided fertile soil for the sexual revolution. The rising prosperity and the financial independence of both sexes made it easier to abandon conventional morality. Taking a mistress or a lover was no longer a luxury reserved for wealthy people. Adultery and cohabitation became more accessible. In the prosperous nations of the twenty-first century, the rapid rise in living standards accompanied a consumerist life-style with widespread hedonism, the endless pursuit of pleasure.

At the same time, at the other end of society, in some countries the welfare state managed by "nonjudgmental" social workers supported unmarried mothers after their serial partners had abandoned them. Hence a joke: God says, *"Thou shalt not commit adultery"*, but the government says, *"It's worth $300 a week."*

Sex Education

Since the appearance of sexology at the end of the nineteenth century, *sex education* directed at children and young people has become an essential component of this revolution. In a liberal approach to sex education, as noted, Scandinavia was already well ahead of other Western nations. However, in 1964, a *secular humanist network* called

SIECUS (*Sex Information and Education Council of the United States*) was founded to promote "value-free" sex education in schools. It has strong links with Planned Parenthood. This nonmoral way of education in sexual matters gradually penetrated some denominational and private schools run by Christians.

In the 1970s, the loosening of sexual ethics in the field of education was also promoted through "values clarification" and a method proposed by the atheist psychologist Lawrence Kohlberg (1927–1987). Using extreme moral dilemmas, students were taken through his "six stages of moral cognitive development", that is, from blindly following rules up to the sixth level of total moral autonomy. Kohlberg's ideal is a person who makes his own morality, having risen above lower levels to become the autonomous individual. Here Kohlberg's ideal comes close to Nietzsche's "superman", who has abandoned conventional morality and risen to a "higher morality". Kohlberg later modified his theory, but when applied to sexual behavior, it becomes yet another element in the revolution.

The Catholic Church first responded to the challenge of secular sex education in 1929, when Pope Pius XI issued *Divini illius magistri*, on the education of youth. In 1965, at the Second Vatican Council, in the *Declaration on Catholic Education, Gravissimum educationis*, the Council Fathers called for a "positive and prudent" education in sexuality.

More guidance appeared in 1981 when Saint John Paul II issued his encouraging exhortation on the family, *Familiaris consortio*. Responding to the 1980 Synod of Bishops on the Family, the pope added "clear and delicate" to "positive and prudent" as qualifying phrases for a good education in human sexuality. He spelled out the rights and corresponding duties of parents, the primary educators in this field. Papal authority encouraged parents to resist attempts to introduce secularized sex education into schools with its program of contraception and abortion.

Guidance for Catholic schools was soon provided by the Congregation for Catholic Education in *Educational Guidance in Human Love*, 1983. Guidance for parents came with finer detail in *The Truth and Meaning of Human Sexuality*, issued by the Pontifical Council for the Family in 1995 at the direction of Saint John Paul II. The title sums up what the Church promotes in the face of distortions: "The *truth* and *meaning* of human sexuality". In 2016, in his exhortation on the family, *Amoris laetitia*, Pope Francis (1936–) maintained the need to provide sound education in human sexuality as a challenge facing Catholic institutions.[1]

Contraception and Abortion for Children

The provision of premature and explicit sex education in public school systems rapidly developed into giving children access to contraception and abortion. I use the term "children" to affirm that at puberty a teenage girl or boy is still a child, responsible to parents, a parent, or a guardian. But parental rights are ignored when a girl can obtain "reproductive health services" behind her parents' backs or when condoms are handed out to teenage boys.

Making it easy to get "reproductive health services" is justified by a pessimistic attitude toward young people: "They are going to do it anyway, so let's make it safe and healthy ..." There is no inkling here that young people may not want to be sexually loose, promiscuous, and irresponsible. However, once you work to get vivid sexual information into the heads of young children, you are

---

[1] See Appendix 2, "Where to Find Catholic Teaching on Education in Human Sexuality".

bound to enter damage-control mode when they enter puberty and adolescence.

In this world of social pessimism, the greatest disease is an "unwanted pregnancy", that is, until the sexually trans-mitted diseases appear. This pessimistic attitude has been absorbed by many social workers, doctors, and nurses, sin-cere people no doubt, but only too willing to undermine parents' rights believing that *"we know better and we are doing so much good."* Here is the self-delusion and smiling hypocrisy of those who service the sexual revolution.

The War against Censorship

Changing attitudes to sexual morality came into public view in the era of the well-publicized struggle to end cen-sorship. It is not surprising that this project was accompa-nied by a widening market for pornography. At the time, no one imagined where that trend would lead.

A leading figure in the fight against censorship in England was the theater critic and producer Kenneth Tynan (1927–1980). Explicitly sexual themes had already appeared in the literature of D. H. Lawrence (1885–1930) and James Joyce (1882–1941), whose works had previ-ously been censored. Now a greater freedom was evident in theater and literature, for example, in the work of play-wright/author John Kingsley (Joe) Orton (1933–1967) and talented American writers such as Norman Mailer (1923–2007), Arthur Miller (1915–2005), and the poet Allen Ginsberg (1926–1997). However, the romantic homosexual novel *Maurice* by E. M. Forster (1879–1970) could be published only after his death.

As with legalized abortion, legislative changes regarding censorship in England had great influence in other nations. The theater, films, television, advertising, and popular music moved in a more explicit direction, first with the treatment of once-forbidden topics, such as homosexuality, then, in the late 1960s and early 1970s, by breaking taboos against nudity, obscene language, and visual material. In 1968, Hollywood replaced the Motion Picture Production Code with a new code classifying films, providing a warning that R or X involved explicit material.

Porno-Power

Pornography has become the major force in the sexual revolution. The eyes and ears are the doors into the mind and heart. The "soft-porn" magazine *Playboy* made millions for its founder-editor, the "high priest of hedonism", Hugh Hefner (1926–2017), that is, before he faced competition from a growing number of pornographic magazines that went far beyond *Playboy*. What was once hidden and restricted now became widespread and normal, apparently starting in Scandinavia. What was once a secret realm with a limited market became a multimillion-dollar industry.

Rapid technological development of the media ultimately has led to *universal access to pornography*. The vectors are not only the mass media, entertainment, and advertising industries, but above all the internet and social media. The material is aggressively explicit, with no topic forbidden, including that dangerous mixture of sex and violence. Women are demeaned and abused, so young males get a perverse message that some of them put into action. The pornographers feed an international industry that does not hesitate to use politics to protect itself and to pursue and punish its opponents.

Wider toleration of pornography, cohabitation, and promiscuity was accompanied by the rise of two ideological and political currents: *feminism* and *homosexualism*.

Women's Liberation

An extreme form of feminism was one of the early results of sexual permissiveness, but many pioneering feminists were not sexually permissive. This may explain certain trends within more recent developments of feminism, for it would not be fair to characterize all feminists as disciples of Simone de Beauvoir. While de Beauvoir, Germaine Greer (1939–), Betty Friedan (1921–2006), and other feminists worked to liberate women from fertility, understood as the instrument of male control, the wider women's movement shows a range of nuanced views, and not always in favor of the sexual revolution.

Feminists rightly oppose pornography, because it demeans women and reduces them to sexual objects who can be tortured or murdered. Some may favor free relationships between the sexes, but only if a woman is not exploited by a man. All feminists are against rape, but they are divided over prostitution. Most see it rationally, as men exploiting women in the sex industry. Others see it as women exploiting men, hence they support the "sex industry". Feminists are generally pro-lesbian, but there is a growing trend in favor of lesbian motherhood, that is, a move away from the childless lesbian couple, hence their support for same-sex marriage.

Contraception is still regarded as liberating, but methods that harm women's health are rejected, and some feminists recognize that male control of women can be exercised by contraception. However, most feminists still support abortion in the name of "choice" and the control of one's body under the slogan "My body, my choice!" This wave of opinion led Ireland to abandon the constitutional restriction of abortion in the referendum of 2018. At the same time, some feminists oppose abortion.

Modern feminism may be more "feminine" and complex, but it still rests on exaggerated individualism, inherited from liberals, or on a violent interpretation of male-female relationships, influenced by Marxist dialectic and de Beauvoir. In the tradition of Margaret Sanger, some feminists work with the neo-Malthusians and their population-control industry, and, serving that cause, they played a key role at the United Nations Conferences of the nineties. On the other hand, there are feminists who question the achievements of the sexual revolution, particularly the illusions of genderism, which I examine in chapter 5. They understand that this social revolution mysteriously suits the controlling power and desires of men.

Gay Liberation

In Judeo-Christian societies, the practices of what came to be called "homosexuality" were never accepted. The Scriptures, Old Testament and New Testament, present human sexuality in terms of male-female relations, contained within and ordered toward marriage, procreation, and the family. This was in stark contrast to societies of the Ancient World where same-sex activity was not understood in moral terms, for example, in ancient Greece and Rome and in the Canaanite societies.

Therefore, in Judeo-Christian societies, homosexuality was a hidden subculture, tolerated in some countries but subject to heavy penalties in others. Wherever same-sex activity was illegal, male homosexuals in particular were victims of violence, blackmail, bullying, exploitation, and brutal remedial treatment, which is why they welcomed the sexual revolution. It helped them to "come out of the closet", to fight to remove discriminatory laws, and to be accepted. What is not well known is that homosexual activity had been decriminalized in France in 1791, during the Revolution. It was gradually decriminalized in various countries in the nineteenth and twentieth centuries. In 1967, male homosexuality was decriminalized in England.

However, in that process, the "gay liberation" of the mid-sixties also turned homosexuality into an ideology, *homosexualism*, with a social and political agenda—defending and promoting an "alternative life-style". Gay liberation thus plays a more consistent role than feminism in the sexual revolution, largely due to activists promoting their life-style, ever fearful of being driven back "into the closet". In the United States, the appearance of gay liberation is usually dated from the Stonewall Riots in New York, in June 1969. In the United States, the martyr symbol of this social movement was the politician **Harvey Milk** (1930–1978), who was murdered in 1978 as he led gay liberation in San Francisco. Stonewall was later taken up as a symbol by English activists led by the actor **Sir Ian McKellen** (1939–).

Going beyond a struggle for rights, homosexualism demands that homosexual behavior should not only be tolerated and legalized, but granted equal legal and social status in terms of *same-sex marriage*. The ideological and political campaign is based on the claim that such behavior is not the fault of homosexual men and women. However, there is confusion at this point over the issue of nurture or nature. Some homosexuals say, "I did not choose to be homosexual" or "I was born this way." Others want to reeducate or recruit the young. That would imply that same-sex activity is learned, not inherited. It is difficult to resolve this question.

As an ideology, homosexualism is often radical and aggressive. Some vocal ideologues vent spiteful hatred on the family, marriage, heterosexuals, religion, etc., and say they want to destroy the whole social order. Along with demands to lower the age of consent, others even defend pederasty and pedophilia, claiming that children benefit from sexual relations with adults. So we are looking at a range of views and different forms of activism.

In the twenty-first century, a "gender" ideology has won favor among homosexual activists, first among some lesbian feminists who argue that one's "sexual orientation" is a form of "gender", that gender is a socially learned role that one can change, choose, or adapt at will. Therefore, Marcuse's polymorphous sexuality should become the norm for everyone. I will examine this recent trend in terms of the now-familiar gender spectrum, LGBTQ. This trend also raises the question of whether the LGBTQ spectrum is helping or harming homosexuals.

Men and women with same-sex attraction who reject a homosexualist ideology resent activist extremists who are provoking reactions of dissension and even *homophobia*. Others know that their life-style carries more tragic personal stories than the superficial "gay" image and pretty rainbow flags would admit. At the same time, the rich and powerful homosexual "communities" found in certain cities favor a perpetual sexual revolution. They seemed undeterred even by the spread of AIDS beginning in the 1980s and monkeypox in 2022. They desperately promoted the theory of "safe sex" secured by way of condoms to protect their own behavior—at any cost. I will examine this tragedy more closely in chapter 7.

Courage

The Catholic Church responds, not by condemning or moralizing, but by proposing the pastoral approach, set out in the Congregation for the Doctrine of the Faith, *Letter to the Bishops on the Pastoral Care of Homosexual Persons*, 1986. The term "disorder" used in the document and in the *Catechism of the Catholic Church* (2357–59) is deemed to be offensive. When considered objectively, it is only a moderate description of deep personal problems that develop out of what is better described as *same-sex attraction*.

Pastoral guidance for men and women with same-sex attraction has developed well, and many resources present a compassionate approach while maintaining Catholic morality.[2] Founded by Fr. John Harvey, O.S.F.S. (1918–2010), a wise American priest whom I knew well, the *Courage* movement and its associated circles for parents and other relatives, *Encourage*, are free from ideology. *Courage* welcomes same-sex attracted people in circles of prayer and care. Contrary to what their critics claim, these movements do not set out to convert, cure, or brainwash men and women with same-sex attraction. On the other hand, Dr. Joseph Nicolosi (1947–2017) applied his faith, skill, and experience in providing reparative therapy with much success.[3] Other groups claim to be able to lead men and women into heterosexuality. It remains an open question whether all their methods are pastorally and psychologically sound. However, that does not justify the aggressive LGBTQ efforts to invent and impose laws that ban these groups and deny some unhappy men and women the free option to seek a change in orientation.

When someone says, "I am gay", the truthful reply is, "No, you are a man [or you are a woman]. So why *define yourself* by one element in your life—that you happen to

---

[2] See Robert Stackpole, *A Bridge of Mercy: Homosexuality and God's Merciful Love* (Stockbridge Mass.: Marian Press, 2018), which includes access to sources on the question of the causes of same-sex attraction.

[3] His books have been banned by Amazon.

have same-sex attraction?"[4] This response strikes at the identity issue in the sexual revolution, when so many people now identify themselves as persons *only* by their sexual orientation. Most human beings do not identify themselves, let alone define themselves, by their sexual orientation. As we shall see, this identity game is being reinforced by an ideological and political power.

Making Vice Normal

By the late twentieth century, the sexual revolution at a broader level had brought a radical change in social attitudes in many countries, that is, by turning what was once considered a vice into a normal activity or even a job. This *reversal of values* has been one of the most pervasive effects of the sexual revolution, reflecting the collapse of sexual ethics at the community level.

The normalizing of prostitution is the main example of this trend. Since her earliest years, the Church has ministered to prostitutes, largely through dedicated women religious who work among the poor, because poverty was the main path to prostitution. The pastoral goal of religious women has always been to liberate, heal, and rehabilitate women and children degraded and exploited by prostitution and sexual slavery. In recent years, in an age of migrations due to wars and economic crises, this ministry has been focused on *human trafficking and slavery*, abuses often perpetrated by international criminal networks that exploit vulnerable women and children, especially refugees.

However, the dishonest language game "redefines" and sanitizes this web of vice, crime, and exploitation. Prostitution becomes the "sex industry" where we find "sex

---

[4] This approach is essential when counselling confused children who are being persuaded that they are "gay".

workers", that is, female and male prostitutes, together with those who manage or control them, no longer to be called madams or pimps. Within the industry, the respectable image of the "escort agency" covers more affluent levels of prostitution, and brothels are transformed into "men's clubs". At lower levels, brothels are concealed among massage parlors. But a social change should also be noted, another effect of the sexual revolution. Having lost their moral compass, some women and men who are not poor choose to work as prostitutes. Sex is just another job, and it pays well.

Arguments in favor of legalizing ("decriminalizing") prostitution run parallel to the legalization of drugs. It was claimed that legalization would end criminal control and assist medical care. But this has not happened. International human trafficking and sex slavery continue, and, worst of all, child prostitution flourishes, funded by sex tourism and largely based in Asia where the exploitation of children feeds off poverty. At the same time in the West, the normalization of underage sex stealthily creeps forward, in spite of the pedophile scandals and the suffering of young victims.

The Pharmaceutical Sex Industry

In a wider sense, the sex industry includes people who own and work in "adult shops" and agencies that sell and manufacture "sex aids" and pornography. But pharmacies are also drawn into this commercial complex.

Aphrodisiacs are supposed to enhance desire or activity. They range from love potions and certain foods and drugs to charms and spells. Aphrodisiacs have always been with us. However, at the end of the twentieth century, sophisticated sexual medication for men came onto the market,

Viagra being the most well-known product. Gradually, the marketing of this sex pill changed from being directed at elderly men suffering from impotence to younger men who have (or think they have) a similar dysfunction. The wide use of this kind of medication reflects a male obsession cultivated by the sexual revolution, and it has been of great financial benefit for big pharmaceutical corporations.

Therefore, in affluent societies, sex has become another profitable commercial commodity. The international sex industry wields political power with ample funds for advertising in all forms of the media. As with the pornography industry, the sex industry punishes those who would thwart its goals, such as groups of citizens who try to prevent its projects in their neighborhoods.

The United Nations Conferences

In the last decade of the twentieth century, the United Nations Conferences became vehicles for promoting the sexual revolution around the world, above all those held in Cairo, on population and development (1994), and in Beijing, on women (1995). As a member of the Delegation of the Holy See at these conferences, I was one of the Vatican foot soldiers, personally briefed for battle and guided by Pope Saint John Paul II.

These conferences not only bring together delegations representing member nations and observer nations. They also include a parallel forum made up of nongovernmental organizations (NGOs), representing a range of interest groups and differing views on the theme of the conference. The NGO forum lobbies the member states at the conference to debate the content of a working document that is released in draft form at the preparatory conference held in New York some months before the conference itself meets. Once the final version is approved by consensus, that document becomes the *program for action*, sent to all the nations as recommendations for new social and political legislation and policy.

The conferences were strongly influenced by the same elements that Margaret Sanger inspired: neo-Malthusians and particularly pro-abortion feminists. The International Planned Parenthood Federation worked with the United Nations Population Fund (UNFPA), allied with feminists and secularist UN bureaucrats from prosperous nations. As we have seen, there is a consistent historical logic in this alliance, bound together by the fearsome myth of an overpopulated world, heading for catastrophe or even human extinction.

We need be under no illusions about the United Nations bureaucracy. The sexual revolution and its culture of death is well represented in the carefully planned programs for action that emerged from Cairo and Beijing. They are currently being pressed into action in many countries through legislation that at the same time transforms each government into a "sexual state". Wherever abortion is "decriminalized", the rhetoric of "women's reproductive rights" in favor of this change comes directly from the program for action of the United Nations conferences of the late twentieth century.

More "effective" population control requires easy access to abortion, sterilization, and contraception, under the cover of "reproductive health" and "women's reproductive rights". To recruit the young for this program, sex education is necessary. Therefore, the word "sexual" must be quietly included in "reproductive rights" to become "sexual and reproductive rights". Words like "family" or "marriage" are to be excluded or redefined.

At the World Conference on Women in Beijing, the feminists attempted to get "sexual orientation" (i.e., the homosexualist agenda) included in the final document, apparently to advance lesbianism. But another project was also pressed. When Hillary Clinton (1947–) arrived in the conference hall representing her husband's U.S. Administration, she repeatedly asserted, "Human rights are women's rights, and women's rights are human rights." I witnessed her tedious mantra. But what was she really saying? *That aborting a baby must become a universal human right.*

This ambitious project emerged and displayed itself dramatically in November 2019. To mark the twenty-fifth anniversary of the International Conference on Population and Development (ICPD) held in Cairo, the United Nations Population Fund organized the Nairobi Summit (ICPD+25) and issued a document revealing the goal of the project: *to make abortion an international human right.* This summit was rigged. It was organized secretly by some pro-abortion nations, and pro-life groups were banned from taking part in it.

However, this time, the United States (under President Trump) and ten other nations broke ranks and exposed the real goal of the Nairobi Summit. They affirmed "there is no international right to abortion", in light of Article 3 of the *Universal Declaration of Human Rights*—"everyone has the right to life." They reminded the summit that the previous conferences had affirmed that abortion should never be used as a method of family planning. The bishops of Kenya denounced the conference as corrupting African youth, and the Vatican refused to participate.

The Nairobi Summit was extended in Paris, from June 30 to July 2, 2021. The United Nations bureaucracy pressed on with its campaign to make abortion a human right, and pro-abortion "world leaders" spoke at the Generation Equity Forum. The President of France, Emmanuel Macron (1977–), hosted the forum. Vocal participants included Hillary Clinton and the U.S. Vice

President **Kamala Harris** (1964–). This time the Vatican was not invited.

Making abortion a human right came before the European Parliament in June 2021. An alliance of socialists, liberals, and greens accepted the "Matic Resolution" by majority vote. This effectively affirms that abortion is a human right and that abortion must be provided on demand. This move beyond "pro-choice" sets up the pro-life movement as religious extremists opposed to human rights. "Women's reproductive health" also endorses eugenics, which could include, for example, exterminating Down Syndrome babies in the mother's womb. The European Parliament cannot bind member nations, but a secularist European society without morals provides a bad model for the United States.

"Women's reproductive health" redefines abortion, no longer as a moral issue, but as an ordinary health procedure. Morality is excluded once aborting unborn human beings is no different from extracting an infected tooth. That lie is reinforced by another lie, the assertion that only "religious people" raise moral issues over abortion. There are, in fact, many atheists and agnostics who oppose abortion on the basis of natural law and irrefutable scientific evidence that life begins at conception. The issues around abortion also highlight the role legislation plays in advancing the sexual revolution by way of the "reform" of laws, the recognition and creation of "new rights", and the familiar pattern of eliminating morality and normalizing vice. *Abortion on demand is an essential element in the sexual revolution.*

5

"Gender": The Revolution Goes Mad

IF WE TAKE THE FRENCH REVOLUTION as the classical model, a revolution passes through a series of phases. First, it fights to seize power, to overthrow the existing system. Then, having gained power, it must consolidate control of the people and ward off counterrevolutionaries or reactionaries. As the revolution consolidates power, the leaders strive to purify its ranks. In France, this purging took the form of the Reign of Terror (1793–1794), when thousands of men and women were murdered, not only aristocrats and devout Catholics, but those who at first had served the Revolution. They were treated as traitors and sent to the guillotine. However, by murdering its own supporters, the revolutionary snake began to devour its own tail. The frenzied madness of the Terror was only terminated by Napoleon's military intervention and his rise to power. Has the sexual revolution entered such a stage of derangement?

It would seem so when we analyze what may be the most bizarre achievement of the sexual revolution, *gender theory* and its aggressive offspring, *gender ideology* or *genderism*. We need to understand the history of gender theory, because its shabby past is not widely known. Ignorance about its origins suits those who promote genderism.

Gender Feminism

In New York early in 1995, I first encountered the mysterious and elastic word "gender". I was a member of the Delegation of the Holy See at the Preparatory Conference for the United Nations Conference on Women, held later that year in Beijing. We were puzzled as to why the word "gender" kept appearing in the draft final document, which was being fiercely debated, paragraph by paragraph, during the Preparatory Conference.

Through a student at Columbia University, we discovered that "gender" was a key term in a new field, *"gender studies"*. The term seemed to come from a group known as Gender Feminists. A feminist "gender" theory had emerged in the dense writings of **Judith Butler** (1956–). Radicals in this circle never use those very bad words *man* and *men*, not even *woman*, preferring *wommon*, or plural *wimmin*!

Butler argues that gender is fluid, that you can change your gender, and this is not simply a choice between two biological sexes, male and female, but rather a series of gender options. She strongly opposes "heteronormativity", that is, describing sexuality in terms of the male-female difference and distinction. Most concerning of all is her advocacy of "child agency", that is, that children should make their own decisions about sex and self-identity. "Queer theory" and "trans theory" focus on the child, which helps explain the current ideological drive to reeducate children by programs in schools focused on changing one's gender and the associated fad of children changing gender.

However, it turned out that an extreme variant of feminism was only one form of a theory with an interesting history and much wider influence, especially now that it has been taken up by many homosexual activists under the familiar rainbow banner, LGBTQ.[1]

Dr. John Money and Gender Theory

The precise terms of gender theory may be traced back to Dr. John Money (1921–2006), a New Zealand psychologist who worked in the United States after the Second World War. He claimed that *nurture not nature* determines our sexual identity, that is, how you are raised and conditioned is what matters, not the nature of your body. According to behaviorist theory, someone born as a boy could be turned into a girl by being raised as a girl—as long as he/she was never informed of his/her true sex.

Money lifted the word "gender" from its grammatical context ("masculine" and "feminine" words in languages such as French and Italian) and then redefined it as *my sexual self-awareness within my mind.* He argued that *this is not necessarily bound to or related to my body and biology.* He believed this helped him treat *hermaphrodites*, people born with some physical characteristics of the opposite sex or those of both sexes.

Money's reputation was tainted by his activities in a bizarre experiment in Canada involving twin baby boys. Having been mutilated during circumcision, on Money's advice one of the boys was raised as a girl. Money forcefully attempted to reinforce this child's female identity or "gender". The child resisted and then discovered his male identity. He underwent surgery to recover his male sex

[1] Useful critical essays on these themes were published by the Vatican's Pontifical Council for the Family in *Lexicon: Ambiguous and Debatable Terms Regarding Family Life and Ethical Questions* (Front Royal, Va.: Human Life International, 2006).

and got married. Then he committed suicide in 2004.[2] His twin brother also took his own life.

Intersex people, once described as *hermaphrodites*,[3] regard Money as a fraud and scoundrel. Nevertheless, Money's supporters of "nurture over nature" continue to press the theory that "gender" is acquired by social conditioning, that it is a "social construct". Certain male/female *characteristics* may be shaped socially by convention, customs, and expectations, but the theory goes much farther with devastating effects, especially in cases of sex change or "gender reassignment".

However, another phenomenon should not be confused with gender transition. Men and women who adopt the clothing and appearance of the opposite sex are **transvestites**. They feel comfortable in the role of the opposite sex, but they are well aware of their biological sex, which they usually accept. At the same time, in the current social climate, some transvestites are drawn into sexual transition.[4] However, transvestism does not necessarily include those actors or entertainers who impersonate the opposite sex.

Postmodernism

In recent years, Money's gender theory and Butler's gender feminism have neatly fused with a third stream,

---

[2] See the 2011 BBC Horizon documentary on Money and his work.

[3] "Intersex" is also used to describe a "gender", those who identify as both male and female. The situation is more complex, as there is also a rare condition known as Androgen Insensitivity Syndrome that affects women who have an XY chromosome.

[4] The final scenes of the "cult movie" *Priscilla, Queen of the Desert*, depict a sad character moving from the transvestite theatrical world toward sexual transition.

Postmodernism, particularly the theories of Jacques Derrida (1930–2004) and **Paul-Michel Foucault** (1926–1984). This philosophy is congenial because postmodernists deny that any objective human *nature* exists. So my "gender" becomes a role that I may select and construct. Moreover, I can change or deconstruct my "gender" because I create my own "narrative". To put it simply, "I am what I *think* I am", or, more precisely, "I am what I *feel* I am." If a man "identifies" as a woman, he is a woman. If a woman "identifies" as a man, she is a man. A person who identifies as both or neither is "intersex", but not in a biological sense. Here the queer theories of Judith Butler come into play.

According to postmodernism, all we can know of reality is words—and words are a means to power. The fluid social construct of "gender" is entered by way of the *choices* of the *autonomous* individual. This choice of my identity is an exercise of "my power".

"*Autonomy*" is invoked to justify not only any sexual choice a person may make but, as in Belgium, the right to euthanasia through suicide, which is regarded as the ultimate autonomous act. But autonomy is a Western liberal myth. As I have already indicated, no one is or ever has been "autonomous". There are no truly autonomous acts. We are all interrelated to one another. Whatever we do affects others, and whatever others do affects us for we are all social beings.[5]

This focus on the autonomous individual partly explains why sex change is described softly as "gender reassignment" and "transition", and "transgender" is preferred to "transsexual". But is gender fluidity scientifically valid? *Can anyone really change his sex?*

---

[5] See Appendix 3, The Problem with "Postmodern" Sex.

On a biological level, no one can change his sex. At the level of human cells, each cell in a male body has the XY chromosome. With rare exceptions, each cell in a female body usually has the XX chromosome. This stamps a person as either male or female, with all the attendant characteristics derived from that biological sex.

On a psychological level, some people change their sexual self-awareness. They identify in terms of what they may want to call "gender". "I identify as a male, so I am not a female." But this raises the question of whether this is delusional, a disorder known as *gender dysphoria* or until recently as *gender identity disorder*. A person with gender dysphoria is alienated from his given biological body, so we hear the assertion, "I am a woman *imprisoned* in a man's body."

Today, the mental health interpretation is politically incorrect. As was expected, gender dysphoria had to be erased from the textbooks. In 2018, under LGBTQ pressure, the World Health Organization removed it from the list of mental disorders and meekly renamed it as "gender incongruence". Then, in March 2019, the World Health Organization removed gender identity disorder from its list of pathological conditions. Yet in the past, psychologists and psychiatrists interpreted gender dysphoria as a deep disorder, even a psychosis.[6]

Like the World Health Organization, the scientific community has also been penetrated and compromised by promoters of nonscientific gender ideology; for example, in 2017 an extraordinary editorial in *Scientific American*

---

[6] This runs parallel to the early twentieth-century interpretation of homosexuality as a neurosis. This has been politically incorrect since the late 1960s, but some would argue that it is a reasonable and moderate explanation for what is called homosexuality, better described as same-sex attraction.

surrendered to the theory.[7] Making science conform to ideology has a shameful history. Distorting and rewriting science in the interests of a dominant ideology was a feature of both Nazi and Communist societies. Here we see the power of the sexual revolution as it enters its manipulative totalitarian phase. *Science must submit to ideology.* When gender theory declares war on the human body, science, informed by evidence and reason, crumbles before political correctness.[8]

Gender-Critical Feminists

However, already we have seen interesting reactions to this trend. Some feminists, such as Germaine Greer, reject gender reassignment projects, particularly the claim that a surgically modified male who puts on a dress becomes a real woman. A collection of feminist essays published as *Female Erasure* criticizes gender theory and ideology because of the harm done to women and children.[9] These feminists are angry about men who do not have surgery and yet "identify" as women.

Transsexuals socially identify with the opposite sex and exemplify true gender fluidity: "I am what I wish to be." In some countries, their passports can bear their chosen gender no matter what sex appears on their birth certificates.

---

[7] Mariette DiChristina and Editors, "The New Science of Sex and Gender", *Scientific American*, September 1, 2017, a triumphalist ideological editorial.

[8] See Pat Byrne, *Transgender: One Shade of Grey* (Melbourne: Wilkinson Publishing, 2018), and *The Little Grey Book on Sex and Gender* (Melbourne: Wilkinson Publishing, 2019).

[9] See Ruth Barrett, *Female Erasure: What You Need to Know about Gender Politics' War on Women, the Female Sex and Human Rights* (Pacific Palisades, Calif.: Tidal Time, 2016). The author brings together a range of critical views, while writing within her own lesbian and esoteric religious perspective.

For marriage, all that will be needed is the passport, no longer the birth certificate. That is all very well until those practical questions arise in the real world: about the use of public restrooms, locker rooms, women's shelters, prisons, and, most controversial of all, when men or women who play sports change their gender.

Now we are hearing other voices criticizing the erasure of two sexes and their replacement with multiple "genders". In 2020, the author of the Harry Potter children's books, J. K. Rowling, stated that she did not agree with transgenderism. She was denounced for her views. In the same year, at Alberta University in Canada, an associate professor of anthropology, Kathleen Lowery, was removed from an administrative position because she views biological sex as "real and relevant". Anonymous students denounced her because she made them feel "unsafe". Academic freedom was crushed by absurd political correctness enforced by that trademark of a totalitarian tyranny, spying and anonymous denunciations.

Gender Ideology: What LGBTQ+ Really Means

From the union between theory and philosophy, *Gender Ideology* has emerged, represented by the familiar letters LGBTQ or variants. Through the Western media, this familiar code has rapidly and mysteriously spread across the world. It has become an effective symbol of *homosexualism*, the ideology that developed during the civil rights struggles of gay liberation in the 1960s. But now LGBTQ *genderism* or *transgenderism* has moved far beyond the basic homosexualist agenda.

LGBTQ "diversity" begins with at least five "genders", but many more may be included in the spectrum, 58(!)

according to *The Weekly Australian*, July 2015, 18–19. The acronym begins with L—lesbians, then G—gay, males or females, and B—bisexuals. So far, this covers certain categories of sexual attraction or orientation. But then there is a fracture point.

The diversity breaks apart when it switches from sexual attraction to the "genders", which are: T—transsexuals or transgender people, Q—queers or questioning, or those who practice gender fluidity, and this seems to be the key category. [I—intersex is sometimes added, hermaphrodites not so much by birth, but by choice. A may be added for asexual, and there is even a spectrum within this category.] So we see that LGBTQ deceives us by fusing and confusing three sexual preferences or attractions, LGB, with an endless series of "genders"—TQIA+.

In the postmodern world view, there is no right or wrong, no inversions or perversions, no sexual neuroses or psychoses, just whatever the autonomous individual chooses or consents to be. In a totally relativistic world, *I choose it. I construct it, so it must be right. I am what I think I am.* That really means "*I am what I feel I am.*" An English man has registered himself as a parrot. After some colorful plastic surgery, Mr. Parrot looks rather convincing. Another man has chosen a gender identity as "a dog", but, so far, we have no details of the relevant surgery.

What is obvious, but confusing, is the way LGBTQ+ mainly describes *sexual preferences or orientations* rather than *sexual difference*, that is, the familiar *male* and *female* categories of human biology. But the spectrum *may* include male and female as two gender poles or as undesirable heterosexual extremes. This is derisively described as a "binary", "two-track", or "heteronormative", understanding of sexuality.

Those who are content with being born male or female are described as "cisgender" to distinguish them from "transgender", those who may wish to change gender. The term "cisgender" is a patronizing attempt to lock everyone into the gender spectrum. But most women and men in this world still identify in terms of their given bodies, that is, biologically. They will have to be "reeducated", starting with the young. They must be liberated from "heteronormativity". They must also use politically correct non-gendered language, never "he" or "she", but "they" or some "new-speak" invented words.

Problems with "Fluidity"

When we ask what those other "genders" TIQ+ mean, LGBTQ+ is also revealed as a demand for total fluidity, a spectrum open to endless changes, like the "polymorphous sexuality" that was promoted by the Neo-Marxist philosopher Marcuse. This is where Q may well be identified as the key gender, and in terms of political action Q seems to be the power base driving LGBTQ+.

Yet there is a big problem here, a fracture point in LGBTQ+. Many male and female homosexuals resent being locked into this "gender spectrum". They resent being used by genderism to promote its unscientific ideology—because *they still identify biologically as male or female*: "I am a gay *woman*, I am a gay *man*." They hold to their "binary" male-female biological identities. Strictly speaking, only L, G, and B are relevant to them.

However, fluidity also contradicts itself. Is there a place on the spectrum to include homosexuals who have chosen to undergo some form of *transition to heterosexuality*? No. In some countries, laws are framed forbidding them to undergo therapy or reorientation programs, all deemed to be illegal. So we fall back on a doctrinaire position: "once gay, always gay", and there you shall remain, no fluidity for you.

As I have already indicated, Christian groups ministering to same-sex attracted men and women are accused of imposing therapy to convert homosexuals into heterosexuals. Some groups and counselors have entered that field, and some therapy is controversial. However, if you believe in inclusive "fluidity" in a democratic society, surely these projects merit toleration. No! Fluidity suddenly has limits, and again we see the intolerance of LGBTQ+ "toleration". No place here for freedom of conscience and freedom of choice, for "once gay always gay", and there you shall remain, whether you like it or not, whether you are happy or not.

When it is probed and deconstructed, LGBTQ+ is also revealed not only as a bullying lobby but even as an instrument of cruelty. Have two vulnerable minority groups, one large, LGB, the other tiny, T, been exploited by LGBTQ+ ideologues? Two questions raise the tough issues.

1. Are homosexual women and men being locked into the spectrum LGBTQ+, whether they like it or not?
2. Are transsexuals being used to change laws and conventions about which they may have little concern? Have they been weaponized, whether they like it or not?

In a deranged ideological phase, are the ideologues and activists of the sexual revolution manipulating and exploiting homosexuals and transsexuals?

In my own country, Australian Marriage Equality (AME) was a political arm of LGBTQ+. This advocacy group hurled accusations of *homophobia* or bigotry against anyone who rejected or even questioned same-sex marriage. However, it is interesting that AME never referred to "same-gender marriage", even though "gender" is now part of modern English usage and the word may appear on forms requiring personal information. Most people still think in terms of two sexes, but they are gradually being "reeducated", and the strategic target is the young, in the schools.

However, in Australia, what was marketed as "same-sex marriage" is in fact transgender or transsexual marriage. So Australians who voted yes in the national survey on same-sex marriage in 2017 were misled. They were in fact voting for much more. This is evident in the new civil papers for marriage, which, under Party 1 and Party 2, provide three options "husband, wife, partner", but to Male and Female is added the mysterious gender identity X. A curious footnote tells us that this can be whatever you wish, which reveals genderism or transgenderism.

Politicians eagerly voting for the new law in Federal Parliament were also misled. Most of them had no idea they were endorsing transgender or transsexual marriages, but once the carefully planned civil marriage papers were published, a major exercise in deceit was revealed, based on sexual discrimination laws.

The legalization of same-sex marriage has forced open the doors of schools to admit genderism. Already, gender theory and ideology have successfully penetrated many schools in Australia through the *Safe Schools Coalition*. The coalition is marketed as an anti-bullying program or the promoter of "respectful relationships" and is a counseling service for students with gender identity issues.

To this strategy may be added an annual propaganda event on May 17 called IDAHAT, *International Day against Homophobia and Transphobia*, "a worldwide celebration of sexual and gender diversities". But legal issues may arise when teachers presume to celebrate this day. A teacher presenting IDAHAT to twelve-year-olds may be accused by parents of "grooming" their children, which is an illegal activity in various parts of the world. Nevertheless, in the United Kingdom, the Stonewall group demanded that LGBTQ+ material be included in *all* subjects taught in government schools, even mathematics!

An LGBTQ+ Victory in the U.S.

In terms of human rights, the LGBTQ+ coalition gained a major success in the United States in June 2020, when the Supreme Court ruled that employment discrimination based on "sex" is not just a matter of female or male, but that "sex" includes sexual orientation and gender identity. Coming after the Supreme Court's recognition of same-sex marriage, the majority decision may well have wider repercussions than simply preventing employers from sacking employees because of their sexual orientation or gender identity.

Obviously, contested cases will arise in this domain, and the problem will be to determine whether the firing was based on sexual orientation or gender identity, and not some other demonstrable reason. The ruling has implications for another contested issue: whether those with traditional moral or religious principles can be forced to employ homosexuals and transsexuals. Faith-based schools are the focus for growing LGBTQ+ pressure in this area, with massive implications for our religious freedom and what that rests upon, freedom of conscience.

LGBTQ+, a Powerful Construct

When we step back and look objectively at the deranged phase of the sexual revolution, an obvious question arises. *But what is LGBTQ+?* Does it really exist? By that I mean, is there an "LGBTQ+ community"? It can be described as a "lobby" that leads politicians and legislators to believe it is a big community, backed by a powerful LGBTQ+ international network, and that it is a united coalition of people spanning the elastic gender spectrum. Is this true? As I have indicated, a deep fissure has opened in the spectrum once we move past the categories LGB. Other practical questions lead to more doubts.

Where do we locate the headquarters of this "LGBTQ+ community"? Where are its offices? Who are its leaders? Are they elected or self-appointed? Who are its official spokespersons? Or is this a successful ideological construct, a string of political lobbies bluffing, intimidating, and misleading millions? And to what extent is it controlled and driven by the radical Q category?

The Pastoral Challenges

Whatever the ideological forces may be, patience and compassion should guide the *pastoral care* of all persons who are caught up in this latest phase of the sexual revolution, above all those persuaded or pressured to seek surgical/hormonal "gender reassignment", including a growing number of children. Encouraging children to change comfortably to their chosen "gender" is part of the program of the *Safe Schools Coalition*. There are also instances when an adult sows the seeds of gender dysphoria in a child. A grandmother dresses her little grandson as a girl. A mother sends her seven-year-old son to school in a dress. Mothers in a baby care clinic refuse to register the sex of their children because "one day they will decide for themselves."[10] But whose choice is that?

Sensitive questions are now being raised concerning children who want to transition. The rapidly rising numbers of these children may indicate that this has become a fad or fashion. In England, this dangerous trend was brought into the open early in 2020 when a psychoanalyst, Dr. Marcus Evans, resigned from the board of the Tavistock Centre, a mental-health clinic in London, since closed, that has a section devoted to gender identity issues. He protested at the fast-tracking of the transitions of children deemed to have dysphoria, when there were other explanations for their requests. For example, the link between autism and dysphoria calls for research. The LGBTQ+ ideologues will have none of this, and scientific caution is crushed by fervent ideology in this latest aggressive phase of the sexual revolution. Once again, *science must submit to ideology*.

As with any distortion of the truth and meaning of human sexuality, the theory, ideology, and practice of gender fluidity can produce bitter fruits—confusion, mental suffering, disrupted families, damaged lives, and personal tragedies, even suicide.[11] The suicide rates for transsexuals are high. Why? The standard LGBTQ+ answer is that these suicides are due to the pressures of "transphobia", that bigots drive transsexuals into mortal despair.

The main reason for self-hatred and suicide is more tragic and deeply personal. It is impossible to change your

---

[10] The pastors of churches that provide infant baptisms are familiar with this argument.

[11] These issues were explored in a fictional English television series, *Butterfly*, tracing personal and family issues that arose when a twelve-year-old boy wanted to become a girl.

sex, and, ultimately, confronting this biological reality has led to despair on the part of some people. They were given high hopes of smooth and easy "transition" by ideologues promoting gender fluidity among other goals.

Banning the Reversal of Transition

However, I return to the other issue of people who want to reverse their transition. LGBTQ+ ideology will not permit that. Therefore, respect for real "fluidity" in the T category is another lie. An English researcher who wanted to study these cases at a university found himself legally impeded. Apparently, this is forbidden knowledge, and, once again, academic freedom must be erased by a domineering ideology.

Pastoral compassion and practical support should be provided for people who regret transition and seek to be "de-transitioned", that is, to revert to their biological sex. As more of these desisters come forward to seek help, their cries must be heard and their sad stories must be told. They reveal that "dysphoria" is much more complex than the LGBTQ+ ideology pretends. Attempts to ignore or silence them will rebound on those who encouraged delusions and brought them deep suffering.

However, even as requests for the return to one's biological sex are increasing, sovereign States are being vigorously pressured by the LGBTQ+ lobby to pass laws, imposing severe penalties, to forbid all procedures to reverse transition. In August 2020, the parliament of the State of Queensland in Australia voted to ban not only the reversal of transition but techniques to reverse homosexuality. Freedom of choice is crushed. Fluidity becomes an illusion. Once "transitioned", there you must remain.

Once gay, always gay, and instructed by an aggressive ideology, politicians have "resolved" what science has never settled—the cause of same-sex attraction. Once again, *science must submit to ideology.*

The Transsexual in Society

In some societies, transsexuals have suffered discrimination and abuse. Some are driven into poverty and resort to prostitution. In India, for example, there has long been a recognized category of men who live as women, usually in sordid circumstances. Nevertheless, in other social contexts, some transsexuals have adjusted smoothly to a new identity. I know of several instances, but each person is well educated and made the transition in midlife, not in childhood or adolescence. They agonized over their identity problem, reflected on it, and sought advice and support. They moved to transition only after a carefully weighed and considered choice to proceed with the demanding steps and stages. It was not easy for them.

These transsexuals are not particularly interested in the cause of those who want to turn them into an ideology and those who seek to target impressionable children. They just want to get on with life. One transsexual has even come forward and questioned the ideology and the enforcement of "nonbinary" language with penalties for "noncompliance", noting that "transsexuals never used to control or compel language."[12]

However, other practical issues will not go away, for example, whether persons who have made a transition

---

[12] Debbie Hayton, "Gender Division", *The Spectator*, December 14, 2019, p. 14.

should serve in the military, in police forces, and other areas of life where crisis conditions occur. This became a matter of debate after then President Donald Trump (1946–) ruled that transsexuals may not serve in the U.S. armed forces. In 2021, this was revoked by President Joe Biden (1942–).

To what extent does gender dysphoria affect the functions of a person's daily work? As already noted, gender transitions raise issues in playing sports, obviously when men who claim to have become women compete as women. This is now a major question in certain sports at the Olympic Games. To this issue may be added those other practical situations in daily life: use of locker rooms, shared bathing facilities, restrooms, women's shelters, and jails.

In spite of these issues, most areas of life and work are open to transsexuals. They are always worthy of respect as persons, bearing in mind their suffering. The Church should accompany them with compassion because there is a vulnerability here that calls for merciful understanding and much patience—but they are being used as a political weapon, and that is yet another cruel injustice.

The Church and Genderism

Notwithstanding a pastoral commitment to accompany men and women, and especially young people, with gender issues, the Catholic Church does not accept gender theory and what flows from it, the ideology of genderism and procedures that implement gender fluidity.

The *Catechism of the Catholic Church* (2332–33) affirms that each man or woman "should acknowledge and accept" his or her biological sexual identity, including "physical, moral, and spiritual difference and complementarity", which "affects all aspects of the human person in the unity of his body and soul". This identity "especially concerns affectivity, the capacity to love and to procreate, and in a more general way the aptitude for forming bonds of communion with others".[13] Whether carried out through sterilization or gender transition, self-mutilation is against the Creator's plan, even as the complexities, confusion, and pressures of gender dysphoria obviously mitigate personal guilt.

In 2015, in Rome, the Synod of Bishops on the Family rejected gender ideology (see text of the final *Relatio*, no. 8). The theory and its ideology also contradict the beautiful *Theology of the Body* proposed by Saint John Paul II.

While he has been pastorally sympathetic to transsexuals, Pope Francis has openly rejected gender theory as undermining sexual difference and differentiation (male-female complementarity in the reciprocal male-female relationship)—hence marriage (see *General Audience*, April 15, 2015). In a specific paragraph in his exhortation on the family, *Amoris laetitia* (56), he gave a trenchant warning on the destructive effects of this theory, its ideology, and practices. He affirmed: "Let us not fall into the sin of trying to replace the Creator. We are creatures and are not omnipotent. Creation is prior to us and must be received as a gift."

On October 1, 2016, in an informal dialogue during his visit to the country of Georgia, Pope Francis said: "Today there is a global war to destroy marriage ... they don't destroy it with weapons but with ideas. It's certain ideological ways of thinking that are destroying it ... we have to defend ourselves from ideological colonization."

Addressing the Pontifical Academy for Life on October 5, 2017, Pope Francis said, "The biological and psychical manipulation of sexual difference, which biomedical technology allows us to perceive as completely available to

---

[13] As cited by the Canadian bishops, July 7, 2017.

free choice—which it is not!—thus risks dismantling the source of energy that nurtures that alliance between man and woman and which renders it creative and fruitful."

In 2019, the Congregation for Catholic Education issued guidelines for schools entitled *Male and Female He Created Them*. The Church's position on genderism was affirmed, but the path of patient dialogue was recommended in response to the rising number of cases of children and young people seeking transition to another sex. Parents should play a key role in gradually and compassionately resolving these situations. In 2020, the teaching of genderism in Catholic schools was ruled out by the new *Directory for Catechesis* (373–78), issued by the Pontifical Council for Promoting New Evangelization.

When we turn to political and social action, we see how "ideological colonization" in gender theory and genderism is happening around us today.

SOGI and the Split in LGBTQ+

Another acronym, SOGI, brings together Sexual Orientation and Gender Identity. SOGI is a combination of the two main components of LGBTQ—LGB and TQ. The political aim is first to force people to unite on the simplified spectrum, regardless of sexual orientation or self-identity. This tactic gives a political impression of great power and unity. If SOGI were to be presented honestly, as with LGBTQ+ it should be split, and it should also be rearranged as GISO, because the real goal is to promote and enforce *fluid gender identity*, GI, and not *sexual orientation*, SO.

This is why men and women who regard themselves as homosexual should not go along with SOGI. Their interest is "Sexual Orientation", not "Gender Identity". If they are content to identify in a "binary" way as male or female, they may have little interest in the gender fluidity ideology driven by the Q category. As already noted, some of those in the LGB categories reject genderism and have openly attacked it. They know well that it is absurd to describe sexual orientation or same-sex attraction as a "gender".

However, they are still being locked into the LGBTQ+ spectrum by those promoting and enforcing fluid Q gender identity. They do not *choose* to become categories in an endless list that forcibly associates them with people with whom they have nothing in common, even some people they may regard as unbalanced or unstable. Moreover, because they see their sex as innate and identify themselves as either female or male, they do not need to get involved in the bizarre gender war that is being waged against the human body. They should recognize that the spectrum has jumped well beyond a liberation movement that secured protection from prejudice and violence. Is LGBTQ+ an exercise of brute power, coercing and punishing anyone who will not fall into line with its ideology?

This manipulation opens two cruel paradoxes. Those who regard themselves as homosexual should reflect seriously on two unsettling possibilities:

1. *Has LGBTQ+ itself become the major cause of homophobia today?*
2. *Is the sexual revolution in its current deranged phase manipulating and exploiting both homosexuals and transsexuals?*

This leads us into the role of the sexual revolution within a much wider political revolution and its global projects for social engineering.

6

Sex in the Wider Revolution

THE GENDER IDEOLOGY reveals the ultimate goal of some activists in the sexual revolution, that is, *the elimination of the sexual identity of the human person*. Once you achieve that goal, radical social and political consequences follow. In effect, you are *redefining the human person*. In turn, that means reshaping the family, marriage, education, society, politics—even religion. Sexual liberation becomes an effective instrument to destabilize, upturn, and change society, to deconstruct social institutions and break down established moral values, leading us into some new political or social order.

At this point, we should begin to see that what we call the "sexual revolution" is a key part of a much bigger and wider revolution that already has its own history and is therefore open to political analysis. This helps us make sense of the hard Left's forceful promotion of the sexual revolution and support provided by sympathizers on the soft Right, especially wealthy people in the corporate world. What has guided this wider revolution?

Who Was Antonio Gramsci?

The sexual revolution has come to play an essential role within the wider Marxist project of a global *social, cultural, and political revolution* envisaged by **Antonio Gramsci** (1891–1937). Few people know his name, so who was he? He was a founding member of the Italian Communist Party. Imprisoned by Mussolini's Fascist government, he died in 1937 after maltreatment in prison. He has had a more enduring influence on the development of modern forms of Marxism than any other ideologue.

Revising Marxist-Leninism and Stalinism, Gramsci argued that the class war and violent revolutions do not work and cannot lead to the triumph of Communism. The real revolution must be social and cultural. It must penetrate and break down *the institutions of bourgeois society*: marriage, family, churches, the professions, legal systems, political parties, corporations, unions, local governments, schools, universities, health care, sports, cultural associations, the arts, the media, etc. The revolution must operate like some invasive insect, stealthily eating out the institutions from within, so that all that is left is a dried-out, fragile shell.

Gramsci himself was interested in a sexual revolution only insofar as women could be liberated from capitalism. His own sexual ethics were traditional. What he provided was a nonviolent revolutionary *method* of undermining what he called the "cultural hegemony", the real centers that control society, the institutions of bourgeois society named above. Together they make up the "hegemony", that is, a dominant capitalist culture that must be penetrated, subverted, undermined, and brought down to liberate people and lead them into pure socialism.

Later his gradual revolution was described as *"the long march through the institutions"*.[1]

---

[1] For a detailed study, see Marc Sidwell, *The Long March: How the Left Won the Culture War and What To Do about It* (London: New Culture Forum, 2020).

The ideology operating to achieve this is described as "cultural Marxism" or a "cultural socialism", which is what we see being propagated in the media, schools, universities, churches, trade unions, and some political parties. The schools and universities are an easy target for they have been described as the "soft underbelly" of our Western liberal societies. It is here that children and young people are won over and reeducated, thus ensuring the future of the ongoing revolution.

The "long march" of the sexual revolution through the institutions that make up a culture has expanded to international dimensions now that the United Nations bureaucracy has thrown its support behind LGBTQ+. This is no surprise. Since the international Conferences on Population, Social Justice, and Women in the 1990s, the United Nations bureaucracy has served as a major force in spreading the sexual revolution by driving social engineering through "progressive" legislation in many nations.

In the Frankfurt School

The emergence of *cultural Marxism* may also be traced to the last years of Lenin when some Communists in Middle Europe came to conclusions similar to those of Gramsci, that violent revolutions do not work. Unlike Gramsci, they broke with Moscow, moved beyond Soviet Communism, and merged Marxism with Freudian psychoanalysis. Stalin hated them and had their key figures murdered. In Germany, in 1923, they founded the influential *Frankfurt Institute for Social Research* to put their adapted Marxist theories into practice. The first director was an Austrian, Carl Grunberg (1861–1940), a Marxist professor of law. Then in 1933, Hitler rose to power, and they were scattered, finding refuge for a time in Geneva and then a secure home at Columbia University, New York.

While they all shared a commitment to a pervasive Marxist social revolution, some in the Frankfurt circle focused on breaking down bourgeois morality and the "authoritarian" family through a *sexual* revolution. In the Frankfurt circle, **Herbert Marcuse** developed his theory and praxis of personal and social liberation through a specific sexual revolution when he was living in the United States. American cultural socialism was later promoted by Saul Alinsky. The Frankfurt School was refounded in 1953, but it moved in a broader direction into a wider range of Leftist causes.

The Libertarians

Now we turn to look at the Libertarians on the democratic Right and the social democratic Left. For a Libertarian, *liberty* rather than liberation is the supreme value, in the form of freedom, civil liberties, human rights, and a democratic society. Throughout the twentieth century, this basic political Libertarianism resisted totalitarianism, Communism on the Left, and Fascism on the Right, and bravely fought these systems to defend democracy.

However, in recent years, many in the wider Libertarian movement have embraced the sexual revolution, so they have been drawn into inevitable collaboration with cultural Marxists. These allies of the cultural Marxists are radical Libertarians or some liberal individualists. In the ongoing sexual revolution, these men and women are more effective and successful activists than people proclaiming hybrid forms of Marxism. To distinguish them from *democratic* Libertarians, whether on the Left or the Right, I refer to them as *sexual Libertarians*.

The sexual Libertarians promote "new human rights" and a total personal freedom, which is now called "autonomy". Those who guided the sexual revolution in its earlier phases were not Marxists but sexual Libertarians: Sanger, Hefner, Kinsey, the advocates of abortion-on-demand and no-fault divorce, together with many non-Marxist feminists and gay liberation activists; for example, Foucault was not a Marxist.

The sexual Libertarian projects are based on the work of sexologists, particularly Kinsey, and focus on the individual and his *inner residing sexuality*, exemplified in the theories of Freud. Sex must be freed from biology, reproduction, procreation, and the boundaries of social convention, religion, and morality, which are protected and maintained in the traditional institutions of marriage and the family.

The sexual Libertarian project today is directed toward the elimination of specific crimes from the law, largely so as to end "all forms of discrimination". Both sexual Libertarians and the Leftists focus on using legislatures to "decriminalize" prostitution, abortion, euthanasia, and drugs. This has immediate impact on attitudes and behavior in a wider society. In the minds of so many people, if something is legal, it is moral, so legalization reshapes social attitudes. "It's legal now, so it must be OK."

At the same time, within the United Nations and major international bodies, the cultural Marxists and sexual Libertarians work to invoke and invent human rights. This will give a cloak of legality to projects that enforce the sexual revolution. The language is familiar: "sexual and reproductive rights".

The Yogyakarta Principles

The major sexual Libertarian project to establish international legal power in the sexual domain was planned and organized at a meeting held in Yogyakarta, Indonesia, in 2006. An impressive array of prominent liberal-minded jurists produced the *29 Yogyakarta Principles*, published in 2007. Ten new Principles were added in 2017, guided by LGBTQ+ genderism, which had asserted itself in the intervening ten years.

This document is the international charter of the sexual revolution. It reveals the goals of the revolution and sets the course to establish legal mechanisms to enforce it. But it has no force in law because it is not an official "international instrument" prepared by governments in the United Nations. It is just a clever "con-job" on the part of a well-organized clique of self-important ideologues.

The *Principles* are all based on the *right to nondiscrimination*. This is the most interesting of all new "human rights". It can be whatever those invoking it want it to be, which is why it is so dangerous. It can be used to destroy established human rights. "You are discriminating against me by refusing to bake the cake for my same-sex marriage."

"You are discriminating against me ..." is accompanied by the now familiar lament, "and I am so offended!" By paradox, Indonesia, the country where the *Principles* were proclaimed, has become embroiled in attempts to impose Sharia Law in sexual relationships with severe application to homosexuals.

Setting the State against the Family, Education, and Religion

In this wider perspective, the sexual revolution is no longer limited to what I have so far described, that is, a series of permissive social trends, building on one another, an accumulative process. It is no longer limited to the ideas and strategies of influential intellectuals and activists. It becomes the key part of planned political projects, legislation, and enforcement, now unfolding among us at local, national, and international levels.

Am I describing a conspiracy? Obviously, conspiratorial elements are evident once we identify the planned stages of the revolution still unfolding in the twenty-first century. But they are "obvious" and "evident", that is, identifiable and visible, so there is no need to subscribe to conspiracy theories. It is enough to return to the neo-Marxists, Gramsci, and the Frankfurt School to identify the method adopted by the sexual Libertarians: relentless penetration and the gutting of the institutions that make up our society.

First, that analysis provides us with a way of judging how far the revolution has succeeded. Secondly, that evaluation in turn should force us to admit the "bad news" that, so far, those committed to this revolution have anticipated, outwitted, and defeated people who reject and resist it. Thirdly, Gramsci, the Frankfurt School, and sexual Libertarians help us understand the strategy and actions of many groups and individuals working today to bring down sexual morality and to establish "progressive" patterns of behavior. Ultimately, these men and women seek to construct a new social order and even a new kind of human being.

The Strategy of Sexual Libertarians and Cultural Marxists

To describe their strategy, we begin in the political sphere, in governments and political parties. Their strategy first aims at breaking down and transforming the *moral authority of the State.* That moral authority has survived wherever governments have protected and preserved the religion and morality of their citizens in natural institutions such as marriage and the family. However, once a government accepts the *Yogyakarta Principles*, then political parties, the legal profession, legislatures, and supreme courts can be transformed into weapons of the sexual revolution. These bodies set official policies and enact and enforce new laws on behalf of the new domineering form of the State.[2]

However, in every society there are three greater moral authorities that can impede the strategies of an authoritarian State. These are:

1. the family
2. educational institutions
3. religion

These obstacles must be undermined or penetrated, changed, and even removed. To achieve this goal, the State itself must become an instrument of change, that is, a weapon to break the moral fiber and influence of the three greater and more personal centers of moral authority in our lives.

The Family

The first target is the family because it is the natural living cell of society. From childhood, families form us in morality, in family and religious values, and through passing on

[2] See Stephen Baskerville, *The New Politics of Sex: The Sexual Revolution, Civil Liberties, and the Growth of Governmental Power* (Tacoma, Wash.: Angelico Press, 2017).

cultural traditions. No-fault divorce strikes at marriage, the basis of the family. To this well-established process of easy divorce may be linked the steady erasure of the rights and role of the father.[3] Families must be reshaped, controlled, broken down by redefining, limiting, taking away or even destroying all parental rights and roles, starting with the father.

We often hear the ideological mantra *"There are many forms of family."*[4] This familiar refrain may suggest moving toward a new social order where ultimately the family can be replaced by "the tribe", where children are raised by a collective, where there is no adultery because marriage has been eliminated and promiscuity is normal. Both parenthood and marriage are eliminated in what may be called a tribal socialism. That may sound far-fetched and even cultic, but a successful assault on marriage and family may logically lead in that direction once State control is assured.

Education and Erasure

The second target running parallel to the family is any center of education. Schools are meant to act for the family, so they must be separated from the family. Parents shall have no say in what is taught in the schools concerning ethics and morality, particularly sex education. Faith-based schools and independent private schools are abolished or absorbed into the one State system. From now on, the State decides everything in the education of the young.

[3] See Stephen Baskerville, *Taken into Custody: The War against Fathers, Marriage, and the Family* (Naperville, Ill.: Sourcebooks, 2007).

[4] The frozen food corporation *McCain's* depicts nontraditional families in its television advertising. [MasterCard and Amazon.com are among the large corporations that feature nontraditional families in their advertising campaigns.]

Here we are confronted by the question: *But to whom does the child belong—to parents or the State?* The neo-Marxists and their allies believe that all children belong to the State.[5]

Universities must also be transformed into centers for ideological change and reeducation. A new wave of intolerance in many universities is a matter of wide concern, not only among social conservatives, but among academics who see their academic freedom replaced by docile conformism to "correct thought". Cases are increasing of academics being sacked, silenced, or punished for teaching politically incorrect ideas or venturing into forbidden areas of research, for example, precise analysis or case studies of gender transition.

A Leftist "cancel culture" or "erasure culture" has emerged, wiping out not only inconvenient ideas but difficult people, for example, the teachers and academics who dare to discuss or promote incorrect thought. As happened in universities under Communism, they become "unpersons". They are mocked and vilified, sacked, and then ignored. At the same time, it is no surprise to see a revival of Marxism on various campuses, all the more dangerous as memories of the millions of victims of the brutal Communist era have also been conveniently erased.

In schools and universities, erasure is also secured when the cultural Marxists rewrite history as did their twentieth-century predecessors, the Soviet thought commissars. In that rewriting, the vindictive nature of a confrontational ideology is also at work. Children and young people are

---

[5] They follow the totalitarians who insist on State ownership of all children, in the past in Germany and Soviet Russia and today in China. Their youth movements, Hitler Youth, Young Pioneers, indoctrinated the young to understand themselves as belonging to the State, whether in the "Volk" or the Party or the Armed Forces, and to spy on their parents for the secret police.

taught to hate the West or to despise their own nation. But what do they mean by "The West"? Judeo-Christian civilization and its cultures and ethical and legal systems are mocked and derided or simply ignored. Going beyond inculcating contempt for their own cultural heritage, even the memories of the past must be erased from the minds of children and young people.

When our historical memory is erased, any organic continuity with our past perishes. Those taught to hate or scorn their own heritage become oblivious to what went before them. Then they no longer know who they are. Robbed of their past, they can be manipulated, reeducated, reconstructed, and controlled.[6] This is an accelerating effect of the culture of "erasure".

Religion

This erasure culture partly explains why the third target, after the family and education, is religion, the most potent vector of culture and memory. All religions must be brought under State scrutiny and control. To achieve this goal, religious freedom is narrowly redefined as *"freedom of worship"*. That is exactly what Communists, Fascists, and Nazis allowed, as if to say to people of faith: *"Yes, you can go to your church, mosque, or temple, but that is all we will permit. After all, religion is a delusion in your head."*

In the religious sphere, these freedoms must be eradicated:

- freedom to express your beliefs in public,
- freedom to quote the scriptures of your religion,

[6] See Pope Francis' encyclical letter *Fratelli tutti* (October 3, 2020), 13 and 14.

- freedom for believers to associate apart from worship,
- freedom to change one's religion,
- freedom to preserve moral confidentiality (e.g., the seal of confession),
- freedom to pass on your faith to your children,
- freedom to run faith-based schools and universities,
- freedom to employ those who will not undermine your faith,
- freedom to influence the wider culture,
- freedom to run hospitals where a pro-life ethical code prevails,
- freedom of conscience for believers working in the medical professions,
- freedom to serve the poor, the suffering, and the marginalized without relying on a socialist system, and, most importantly,
- freedom, when required, to challenge and oppose the State on moral grounds.

Killing Democracy

Once you turn the State into an instrument of social-engineering, you mount an assault on *democracy* itself. The democratic State becomes what is now being called an "authoritarian democracy" or an "ideological democracy". We see this happening when decision-making is transferred from legislatures elected by the people to various courts, tribunals, and other agencies of change, such as government departments, bureaucrats, State media experts, social workers, and politically correct consultants. Canada is moving into this distorted redefinition of democracy. The United Kingdom risks taking the same road to soft totalitarianism.

The people may still vote, but that is where democracy begins and ends. A conformist ideology invoking "consensus" or "community values" takes over, driven by those who are "woke". Their smug ideology is currently called "political correctness". I prefer to describe it as the *fascism of the mind*. Those who will not conform to the "social consensus" are erased or, as Pope Benedict described this trend, they are punished by being socially "excommunicated".[7]

The assault on freedom of speech and democracy by the "cancel culture" or "erasure culture" has been challenged by a Libertarian circle, some with Leftist sympathies, who warned about the trend in an open letter.[8] They wrote in the context of the social upheaval of the violent street demonstrations in 2020. They warned about what happens when political correctness takes control and erupts in aggressive acts. The anger of street demonstrators is irrational, emotional, and assertively dogmatic. It has become a kind of religion for those who are "woke".

Analyzing the sexual revolution as a radical Libertarian project, the German sociologist **Gabriele Kuby** (1944–) has argued that this is the *"destruction of freedom in the name of freedom"*.[9] This inversion is not new. In the French Revolution during the Terror, when the Girondins or moderate revolutionaries were being sent to the guillotine, one prominent victim was **Madame Marie-Jeanne Roland** (1754–1793). On her way to the scaffold, her words of reproach to the Jacobin radicals about to kill her resound

---

[7] Pope Benedict in an interview, published in the final chapter of his biography, *Benedict XVI: A Life*, by Peter Seewald.

[8] "A Letter on Justice and Open Debate", in *Harper's Magazine*, July 7, 2020.

[9] See Gabriele Kuby, *The Global Sexual Revolution: Destruction of Freedom in the Name of Freedom* (Brooklyn, N.Y.: Lifesite/Angelico, 2015).

across the centuries: "*O Liberty, what crimes are committed in your name!*"

Fear and the Killing of Hope

Along with politically correct assaults on human freedom, we also observe another crime against the young, the *killing of their hope in the future*. In neoliberal free-market societies, many young people and children now look into the future with fear and dread. A teenager scolded adults at the United Nations, and thousands of children and young people demonstrated in the streets to announce impending ecological catastrophes, nothing less than human *extinction*. The global pandemic of 2020 reinforced this fear among many young people.

However, a collision between generations has been engineered. Encouraged by the media and various teachers and professors, many young people voice their misery and discontent. But this should not be so. Did not sexual freedom with the endless choices of consumerism bring these young people heaven on earth? Why, then, are so many of them angry, depressed, even despairing?

An impending catastrophic future has long been a theme in science fiction and futuristic novels. Now it also enters the minds of adults through the imaginative media. *The Handmaid's Tale* depicts a fantasy future when male religious conservatives oppress women in a totalitarian nation. This implausible future scenario also functions as a potent pro-abortion myth.[10] After 2020, the fear of an imminent dystopic future among adults has been

---

[10] See Peter J. Elliott, "The Handmaid's Myth", in *Quadrant*, November 2019, an analysis of the novel, the film, and the television series.

reinforced by the global COVID health crisis and its economic challenges.

But Who Pays?

When considering the sexual revolution, my Italian friends would raise the crucial question "*Ma chi paga?*"—*but who is paying for it*? All revolutions cost money. The sexual revolution needs big finance, provided by key movements, organizations, companies, and some wealthy individuals. One interesting patron has been the Hungarian billionaire George Soros (1930–). In the context of his well-known Libertarian support for "a free and open society", he funds some causes in the sexual revolution together with the decriminalization of drugs. Funds flow to specific causes from his *Open Society Foundation*.

In some ways, this revolution is "self-funding". As already indicated, huge sums are generated by the pornography industry and the sex industry. But the sources are not necessarily soiled. The gender feminist Judith Butler has received ample financing for her work from prestigious sources. Respectable secularist foundations also provide money for *population control* by way of abortion, sterilization, and contraception. For example, the *Ford Foundation* and the *Rockefeller Foundation* fund International Planned Parenthood. Money from various sources poured into Ireland to help gain same-sex marriage and then to bring down the constitutional restriction on abortion.

However, once any government succumbs to the revolution and becomes the instrument of ideological social engineering, our taxes can flow readily into the sexual revolution, funding causes, groups, institutions, and organizations that eagerly claim more and more State subsidies.

This is another success of the "long march", the prized spoils of campaigns waged to change legislation and to shift control and decision-making to unelected tribunals and agencies of change. All those government departments, the bureaucrats, State media experts, social workers, and politically correct consultants must also be subsidized by our taxes. Then they live off us, and so we feed the ongoing sexual revolution.

Their Goals

When we bring these currents together, we should see that the sexual revolution is a major component in that wider social revolution, originally envisaged by the Marxists, Gramsci, and the Frankfurt School, but brought to success by sexual Libertarians. The role of the sexual revolution in wider social change may be demonstrated by listing its major goals and achievements and by reflecting on the effects in our society and our lives today.

In a wider politically correct context, it is socially "progressive" to reshape our lives through, for example:

- *abortion as a human (women's) right,*
- *abortion on demand,*
- *abortion up to birth,*
- *abortion to eliminate "inferior" people (e.g., Down Syndrome babies),*
- *embryo experimentation,*
- *cloning,*
- *commercial surrogacy,*
- *abolition of paternity (so fathers no longer exist in law),*
- *value-free sex education of children,*
- *same-sex marriage,*

- *same-sex adoption,*
- *same-sex fertility treatments,*
- *banning conversion therapy for unhappy homosexuals,*
- *universal access to gender reassignment,*
- *gender reassignment of children,*
- *"safe schools" programs teaching gender ideology,*
- *LGBTQ+ ideology in all school curricula,*
- *legally abolishing the words "father" and "mother".*

Other familiar projects may be added:

- *euthanasia, beginning with assisted suicide,*
- *legalization of all drugs, starting with cannabis,*
- *elimination of religion in schools,*
- *religious freedom restricted to "freedom of worship",*
- *inventing new "human rights",*
- *and the total autonomy of the person ...*

The Catholic Church rejects this program because it is contrary to life, justice, and human freedom. It is an assault on the nature and dignity of the human person. For the same reasons, the Church rejects totalitarian ideologies on the extreme Left and the hard Right. This has been embodied in our consistent social doctrine.

The Soft Right

However, in most political parties, we find men and women who serve the "progressive" social revolution because it seems to be attractive. It is inclusive, tolerant, and so politically correct. Led on by the slippery right to nondiscrimination, many cultural Libertarians have fallen into this category. This is why the term "bourgeois

revolution" may well encompass many naïve people on
the soft Right who serve the process envisaged by Gramsci
or the Frankfurt School. In the era of the Cold War, the
Communists called them the "useful idiots". The expression has not dated.

Today, some of these people would be furious were
they to be told that they are associated with Marxism or
"The Left". Yet, in neoliberal free-market societies, some
leading capitalists support the same-sex marriage cause,
openly endorsed by major corporations. They happily display rainbow flags and include LGBTQ+ themes in advertising, persuaded that there is a lucrative "gay market" out
there. Many of those involved cannot see that they are
being manipulated by expert operatives who know exactly
what they are about, working away to achieve their goals
on the "long march through the institutions", now erupt-
ing as the aggressive cult of the "woke".

Toward a "New World Order"?

But what is their ultimate goal? It is no longer some perfect Communist society, the socialist utopia envisaged by
Marx, Lenin, Stalin, and Mao. That fantasy faded when
the Soviet system imploded, when its empire fell apart, and
when Communist China absorbed capitalism into what
might be called "corporate communism".

The earthly paradise shaped by the alliance of sexual
Libertarians, secularists, commercial interests, and neo-
Marxists would be a world of enforced political correctness,
a world without freedom of speech, a world where many
of us would have no place at all—after being "erased".
It would be a totalitarian society, but not in an obvious
way, which is why I do not interpret "new world order"

in any paranoid political categories.[11] It would be "nice", enticingly comfortable. This secularist world would seem to be a "tolerant" society, sweetly "inclusive", "diverse" and "sustainable", to use three favorite words in the overworked jargon that is fashionable among the "woke".

But what kind of human being is being fabricated for this "new world order"? *Transhumanism* is the term used for the construction of a new kind of person. This is where the mysterious Q gender of the current phase of the sexual revolution comes into its own and requires further study.

Nevertheless, to achieve this goal, everyone must come under closer scrutiny, hence State control.[12] This is evident as the People's Republic of China moves to install enough cameras to observe and record the faces, words, and actions of every citizen everywhere. China is not the only emerging "surveillance State" where all people can be scrutinized, monitored, and controlled by the accelerating technology of surveillance. At the same time, people are manipulated by media that are directed by smiling "coercive utopians". But can any promised earthly paradise or "utopia" be achieved by coercion?

There are subtle forms of coercion. The promise of the "good life" entices people to become captivated by materialist substitutes for religion built around the good things in life, such as comfort, leisure, fine foods and wine, sports, tourism, cruises, and entertainment. This is where the corporations and service industries come into play, and, in that context, sex is another commodity to market.[13] Pleasure and comfort provide the dominant meaning of

---

[11] But it is interesting that the expression "a new world order" came first from Adolf Hitler.

[12] See Pope Francis' encyclical *Fratelli tutti* (October 3, 2020), 42.

[13] See Mark Regnerus, *Cheap Sex: The Transformation of Men, Marriage, and Monogamy* (New York: Oxford University Press, 2017).

life in a "globalized" world. This is already happening all around us, so we must ask—is such a "new world order" inevitable?

It is not inevitable. In this century, I believe its rise will be checked by resistant religions and traditional cultures, even certain nations holding to values based on the family, faith, and tradition. Resurgent Islam will never endorse it. Traditional Jews and Christians reject it. Democratic Libertarians are already turning against it. However, the best means of a positive resistance will be proposed in the final chapters of this book. First, we need to step back and reflect on what the sexual revolution in a wider social movement has achieved.

7

A Harvest of Suffering

THE VISIBLE ACHIEVEMENTS and human effects of the sexual revolution make up a challenging list. The breakdown of marriage and family life has been facilitated by:

- legislation favoring easy divorce;
- cohabitation in place of marriage;
- legalized homosexual marriage;
- the adoption of children by homosexuals;
- the continuing spread of AIDS;
- a less-publicized resurgence of other venereal diseases, STDs;
- the open promotion of variations such as sadomasochism;
- permissive sex education aimed even at small children;
- prostitutes redefined as "sex workers";
- the increase of "sex-change" surgery for transsexuals;
- puberty blockers and other transsexual medication for children;
- transsexual surgery for children and adolescents;
- men identifying as women who compete in women's sports;
- increased sexual harassment;
- more rapes, more domestic violence toward women;
- the persecution, vilification, and erasure of those who resist changes;

- and always more pornography for everyone, including small children ...

Political correctness tolerates every sexual variation, while making some noises against the violence. Yet even here, the bottom line is *free choice, mutual consent, and not harming anyone*—unless they "choose" and "consent" to be harmed! This sounds persuasive until reality hits us in terms of the natural world in which we live. Factors in the human body that are beyond our control have already confounded permissive behavior, and we need to examine them.

AIDS, STDs, and "Safe Sex"

In 2020, most of the world was locked down by the coronavirus pandemic, which took the lives of many people in various nations. But looking back to the final decades of the twentieth century, we see a different disease with a more specific cause and focus. This affliction shook the victories of the sexual revolution. We were confronted by the lethal effects of unbridled sexual freedom in terms of a threat to the lives of men, women, and children.

History is again instructive. Diseases derived from or associated with sexual activity have been with us for centuries, and, until recently, they were known as *venereal diseases*. Today, the main diseases in this category are human papillomavirus (HPV), syphilis, gonorrhea, and chlamydia. Developments in medical science in the twentieth century have checked these diseases, which are now known as *sexually transmitted diseases*, STDs, together with *sexually transmitted infections* (STIs), such as herpes. However, the U.S. Centers for Disease Control and Prevention reported that annual cases of STDs reached an all-time high for the sixth consecutive year in 2019. Although cases decreased in the early months of the pandemic, infections rose again by the end of 2020, with cases of gonorrhea and syphilis exceeding 2019 levels. Logically, this trend indicates that more irresponsible sexual activity is the cause of the increase of these diseases.

However, in 1981 a new STD was identified in the United States: HIV/AIDS. A human immunodeficiency virus (HIV) leads to Auto Immune Deficiency Syndrome (AIDS), a collapse of the auto-immune system, which in turn leads to other conditions that cause death, such as cancer. This disease had been developing over many years, and some theories as to its origins focused on a species of African monkeys. What is more important is how it is passed on between people.

The main way HIV/AIDS is transmitted among humans is through the transfer of bodily fluids during sexual acts, particularly male homosexual activity. HIV/AIDS is also passed on through unsterile injections, for example by reusing needles, hence its prevalence among some drug addicts.

Unfortunately, the scourge of AIDS has not been halted by well-funded research and sophisticated new medication. Life expectancy among victims may have been extended, but at present there is no cure for AIDS. Here, we enter another delusionary zone of the sexual revolution, the dangerous myth of "safe sex".

"Safe Sex" or "Safer Sex"?

Once the disease was identified, campaigns were initiated to limit its spread by the use of the condom, which was claimed to be the effective barrier to infection when employed in homosexual or heterosexual activity. We were told that the condom provided "safe sex". To a large extent, this is true. The condom does reduce transmission, if used properly. But as surprise pregnancies and recourse to abortion show, the condom is not a perfect contraceptive. Then how can it be a perfect antidote to AIDS? So is there such a thing as "safe sex"?

This issue generates emotive controversy. Campaigns for "safe sex" based on condom use also reveal the determination never to give up sexual activity, particularly on the part of those homosexuals who are promiscuous. The only politically correct word that places a limit on their sexual activity is "safe" or, for the better informed, "safer". The condom may render sexual activity safer, but it does not make sexual activity safe if the goal is to prevent the transmission of AIDS and the other STDs. In fact, a false security may encourage increased promiscuity. There may even be a strange reaction that scorns consequences by taking risks.

At one stage, the struggle against AIDS was even romanticized into a kind of "war", with a cult of victims who were depicted as brave warriors.[1] However, AIDS is always a tragedy. It is marked by intense human suffering, calling for compassion for its victims and support for those who love and care for them at home or in hospices. Urged by the charity and mercy of Jesus Christ, the Catholic Church continues to provide palliative care for victims of AIDS.

These men and women are the most obvious victims of the sexual revolution. It killed them. Prominent among them was the postmodern philosopher Paul-Michel Foucault. His book *The History of Sexuality, the Will to*

---

[1] A rainbow shrine to this romantic distortion of a tragedy was set up at a side altar in St. John the Divine Episcopal Cathedral in New York; good intentions, sad outcome.

Knowledge (1976) had some influence in the sexual revolution. His promiscuous life-style destroyed him and the young men and boys he infected. He did not seem to care.

The only effective response to AIDS and to all STDs is a real change of behavior through self-control. That involves discipline, self-sacrifice, and the choice of chastity and fidelity. Such responsible behavior prevents transmission of AIDS and other STDs. By behaving responsibly in the early months of the pandemic, people showed they could discipline themselves in the face of risk.

The Collapse of Personal Morality

The tragedy of AIDS reveals how responsibility, duty, and sacrifice have been turned upside down by the sexual revolution, so that:

- "responsible" parenthood means resorting to contraception, sterilization, or abortion—to prevent babies at any cost;
- "duty" means tolerating everything and everyone, including one's unfaithful spouse or promiscuous children;
- "sacrifice" means giving up the husband, wife, or children you love because your spouse "moved on" or obtained an easy divorce in the name of "family law"—or even gained a divorce online.

Moral language is permitted only in a soft romantic way: "loving", "caring", "sharing" become "values" that make any form of consensual sex "appropriate" or even necessary. There is no concept of normalcy. Fornication becomes premarital sex. Virginity is ridiculed as immaturity. Morality is reduced to a private feeling because there is "your morality" and "my morality". Each of us is autonomous. We should also note that "values" are what I choose to place on something, that is, they are subjective and flexible. What I value you may not value.

Abortion and euthanasia are stripped of any moral meaning and become merely private "medical procedures" to which everyone has a right of access. Legislation is sought to make all hospitals provide abortions, and doctors must either be prepared to carry them out or refer mothers to other doctors who have been trained to kill the unborn. In some nations, extreme abortion laws now permit abortion up to birth.

As romantic sentimentality replaced traditional morality, generations emerged in the "developed countries" with no sexual ethics at all. The first signal of this moral vacuum may well have been the catchy line from *Love Story*, a sentimental 1970 book and film—"*Love means never having to say you're sorry.*" Really? Just think about that assertion, particularly if you are married. Christians and Jews could respond that "Love means *always* having to say you're sorry." But reality is inverted in a world of illusions and delusions where everything is relative and the autonomous ego rules.

When Christians Surrender

Vulnerable to the permissive culture emerging around them, some liberal Christians soon compromised with the sexual revolution. In the mid-1960s, the attractive situational ethics of Joseph Fletcher (1905–1991) influenced some liberal Protestants, who began to proclaim a "new morality". Fletcher had been an Anglican clergyman, but he later declared that he was an atheist. In Fletcher, we find sentimental subjective love used to justify a range of key features in the sexual revolution.

Situational ethics helps explain why some liberal Protestants and Anglicans endorse same-sex marriage. Submitting to the subscientific doctrines of gender fluidity, the Church of England provided a service of blessing, a quasi-baptism, to celebrate completed transition from one "gender" to another. But the Catholic Church has also been penetrated by the sexual revolution. For example, some Catholics have also surrendered to the LGBTQ+ ideology and its concrete agenda. One factor behind this trend is a shift in moral theology that followed the Second Vatican Council.

Related to situational ethics, indeed, inspired by its suggestion that the end justifies the means, the "consequentialism" of certain European and American Catholic moralists such as **Franz Bockle** (1921–1991) and **Charles Curran** (1934–) spread among seminaries and theological faculties. Consequentialism was welcomed by those liberal Catholics who were already dissenting against the teaching of Saint Paul VI on contraception in *Humanae vitae*.

In his lucid encyclical *Veritatis splendor* (*The Splendor of the Truth*), Saint John Paul II rejected this decadent moral theology, for example in section 75 on consequentialism. He set out a program for renewing Christian morality at the personal and social levels. In spite of vigorous papal efforts to refute a relativist approach to morality, whether on the part of Saint John Paul II or Benedict XVI, consequentialism lingers on in some theological faculties, and a spirit of tolerant relativism still spreads in the Church, particularly among middle-class Catholics in prosperous secularized societies. The word "values" is invoked, sometimes dressed in Christian garb as "gospel values".

As noted, in the 1970s in some countries, Catholic education was influenced by the theories of the American psychologist Lawrence Kohlberg. That this happened so easily indicates how quickly the classical morality of the Natural Law, moral precepts, and the virtues had been replaced by fashionable situational ethics. The systematic approach of old-style casuistry was replaced by the new casuistry of liberal Catholic moralists. Casuistry is resolving moral issues on a case-by-case basis, applying traditional Judeo-Christian ethical principles. But its new form applies the fluid values of a new morality. This process becomes one of finding loopholes to justify departing from traditional moral norms.

Situational ethics and consequentialism are still favored among small but vocal reform or "renewal" groups of elderly middle-class Catholics. They fight an online civil war within the Church, shamelessly exploiting the past failures of bishops to stop pedophilia. Their dissent is complemented by those Catholic politicians who publicly reject Church teaching on abortion, sexuality, marriage, and euthanasia. These men and women still display membership in the Church when it suits them. Naturally, they are favored by the media as they spread much confusion.

Dissenting priests also soothe the consciences of those prosperous Catholics who never want to be out of step with their friends, whether around the dinner-party table, in the boardroom, or at the tennis club. I would argue that such dissenting Catholics are themselves ignorant puppets of the sexual revolution.

Wider Decadence

The war against conventional morality has moved to the stage where "conventional morality" has become a derisive description of the values held by "people of faith" and other social conservatives. But, if the swing to same-sex marriage is any indicator, "conventional" morality has changed into a conformist permissiveness, reflected in changing public attitudes that play an important role in advancing the sexual revolution.

In the United States, a turning point was the reelection of President Bill Clinton (1946–) which revealed public indifference to the sexual behavior of presidential candidates, a factor that a few years earlier could have cost him the election. But that softer view would later begin to crumble in light of sexual harassment accusations directed at politicians and media celebrities. However, strong vectors of permissiveness are operating in our societies, and it is helpful to review some key areas.

The media continue to be a major influence in changing people's values and life-styles. Media celebrities set the tone for sexual adventures in the suburbs. The bored wife who launches into adultery or who experiments with lesbianism may well model herself on glamorous personalities who inhabit her virtual world of erotic delusions.

Media corporations glamorize promiscuous (and shallowminded) characters in the widely acclaimed TV "sitcoms" *Friends* and *Sex In the City*. Marriage is trivialized through social reality series such as *Married at First Sight* or through the fantasies of a "love island" where couples play at being Adam and Eve. The media also make homosexuality acceptable as just another "life-style", not only by promoting popular homosexual celebrities, but through wellcrafted romantic films, one even glorifying pederasty.[2] A

[2] For example, a 2017 film "acclaimed by critics", *Call Me by Your Name*, depicts a relationship between an adult male and a seventeen-year-old boy, criminal activity in many countries. Deceased media pedophiles such as Jimmy Saville are condemned, but, until recently, the bizarre activities of Michael Jackson have been explained away.

controversy erupted over the Disney Corporation targeting children with appealing LGBTQ+ characters.

The social media are a more recent development, literally placing access to pornography in the hands of everyone. In 2020, it was estimated that forty million U.S. adults regularly view pornography via the internet and that many teens and children are also viewing pornography. The viral crisis of 2020 saw many resorting to pornography in the time of domestic confinement and lockdown.

At the same time, sexual predators exploit the various forms of social media to gain access to children and young people. Parents raise issues of bullying and cases of suicide or self-harm, often involving sexual harassment or seduction. Families, the police, and judicial systems struggle to provide justice and protection for vulnerable victims.

The advertising industry is another virtual world of glamour and attractive fantasies. For many years, advertising has used sexual imagery to attract customers—usually men. In the late twentieth century, this strategy became more explicit and even foolish, to the point where the product being promoted vanished amid efforts to shock or entice customers with erotic novelty or thinly veiled obscenities.

The world of popular entertainment continues to provide an explicit vector of sexual permissiveness. The stand-up comedians who captivate young adults range from gifted clowns down to disorderly men and women whose repertoires depend on repeating obscenities again and again loudly, even while pretending to be drunk or drugged. Mockery of religion and blasphemies are included in these "daring" acts. After a while, such comedy becomes as predictable as those tedious film scripts that blast us with four-letter words.

This assault on human dignity and decency is designed to wear us down. In the end, we are no longer shocked or numbed, and that is what was intended all along. This is another strategy to break boundaries and create "tolerance" and indifference. This is the *normalization of obscenity*.

Fashions in dress for women and men have obviously been reshaped by the sexual revolution, which scorns the Judeo-Christian insistence on modesty. For centuries, phases have come and gone in which some fashions threw aside conventions of body privacy and modesty. But this trend has reached bizarre levels and spread so widely that what once shocked people has become "cool", especially among the young. Immodesty has been normalized. One fashionable clothing company uses a familiar obscene word to sell its products—and no one cares.

The "New Age" movement continues to offer people religiosity without morality and spirituality without ethics. As indicated, with its nineteenth-century occultist roots, this curious form of decadence appeared in the 1960s with the psychedelic pop culture and the "Age of Aquarius". New Age superstition also tends to mysticize permissive sex through the more sinister elements in Eastern religions, such as sexual yoga, hence revealing that its roots lurk in the occultist swamp of the late nineteenth century.

Impact on the Family

However, it is *the family*, above all, that bears the brunt of the sexual revolution. Permissive projects and legislative strategies strike at marriage and break apart families, leaving wives/mothers and husbands/fathers abandoned, and a horde of wounded, confused children, some of them delinquent, drug-addicted, and promiscuous. This is a harvest of broken lives: men and women hardened in vice, hence cynical and despairing of life; children old beyond their years; women and girls bearing the deep personal scars of abortions, macho manipulation, and betrayal, the victims of male lust that posed as love and then erupted in domestic violence.

The abandonment of marriage has been a surprisingly rapid effect of the sexual revolution in many countries. Couples no longer marry, choosing instead to live together in a variety of arrangements, either in a stable relationship or in a series of relationships, a kind of serial cohabitation. What is really happening? This is a choice to avoid *commitment and responsibility*, to evade being bound or tied to another person, legally or morally. Children are the first losers in this ever-shifting grown-up world of "partners" and serial relationships. But who wins out in these relationships?

Cohabitation is mainly a man's game. He is free to move in, move out, and move on. Some women may benefit from cohabitation, particularly in cases when the man is awarded custody of the children. Not all struggling single parents are women. But cohabitation is predominantly a man's game.

Domestic violence is usually, though not always, caused by men, and the victims are women and children. But the ideologues insist on renaming it. Domestic violence becomes *"family violence"*, insinuating that the family is to blame, that the family is the cause of violence against women and children. This standard Marxist principle was promoted by Marcuse, who argued that the family is an oppressive bourgeois institution. While the term "family violence" may have a specific limited meaning in some cultures,[3] we should always insist on using the neutral term "domestic violence" when we work to heal and reduce this scourge.

---

[3] As in cases when a family persecutes a woman over a dowry dispute.

Legalized same-sex marriage is impacting the family. We were told that there would be "no consequences", and now the struggle is on because the consequences are with us. Because a same-sex couple cannot describe themselves as a "mother and father", in France the terms "father" and "mother" are banned from school admission forms. This follows England and Wales, where the terms "father" and "mother" were banned from admission forms in Catholic schools following a complaint that the words "discriminated against" gay parents and stepparents. The terms now become "parent 1" and "parent 2" in France and the UK. But if you catch up with fertility treatments, you can have four parents—legal mother, donor father, legal father, and birth mother. To this may be added the assault on religious and academic freedom, particularly directed against traditional believers who reject same-sex marriage and the LGBTQ+ agenda.

Easy access to abortion has had devastating effects on families. When prenatal tests identify unborn children with Down Syndrome, some doctors press the mothers to abort their little ones. A human being is killed, a woman bears the guilt, and the medical profession steadily decays as the new eugenics seeks out and destroys small humans who are guilty of the sin of being imperfect.

Pope Francis called this practice the "white glove" equivalent to Nazi eugenics. It has been very successful in Denmark. But pro-life activists standing outside abortion "clinics" are criminalized for offering to counsel women. Legislation that is supposed to prevent these women from being harassed has had another effect. *The abortionist is now a protected species*, but pro-life doctors are vilified. Around the world, as already noted, we see new barbaric abortion laws that permit *abortion up to birth*, for example, in New Zealand, introduced just as the viral pandemic arrived.

As these trends show, easy access to abortion is the most spectacular inversion of morality brought about by the sexual revolution.

Pedophilia

Nevertheless, one last barrier to total permissiveness *perhaps* remains: the *sexual abuse of children* through pedophilia, pederasty, prostitution, or child pornography. A legal rejection of active pedophiles still holds, thanks to international efforts by governments, the police, and victims' action groups, but in practice the sexual exploitation of children continues and is well protected through criminal networks.

In the Catholic Church and in other Christian communities, we have been confronted and shamed by the harm done to so many innocent victims and the erosive effects of pedophile crimes committed by clergy and religious. Naïve or incompetent bishops and religious superiors allowed this to happen, moving the perpetrators on, concealing their crimes, and sometimes listening to psychologists who mistakenly claimed that pedophilia is curable.

Within the Catholic Church in the United States, statistics for offenses by clergy and religious seem to peak in the 1960s and 1970s, that is, at the very time when the sexual revolution gained its major victories. However, this was also the time of the liberalization and loosening up of Catholicism after the Second Vatican Council. There was a campaign against celibacy, evident in books with titles like *The Sexual Celibate*, and there was even talk of a "third way" between marriage and celibacy. Saint Paul VI reaffirmed celibacy. His vision was later developed in a positive marriage perspective by Saint John Paul II. But much damage had been done, and efforts to break down celibacy continue, particularly in bureaucratic German Catholic circles.

However, celibacy has not been identified as a *cause* of pedophilia. Obviously, no active pedophile is a celibate. Many abusers are married or living in "a relationship". What can be argued is that the permissive environment, in society and in the Church, has made it easier for the perpetrators to conceal or rationalize their abuse.

In February 2019, the retired **Pope Benedict XVI** (1927–) voiced his conviction that the sexual revolution, by corrupting moral theology and endorsing homosexual cliques, was a driving force in the scandals that have battered the Church. He did not hesitate to go to the atheist factor in the sexual revolution and the collapse of morality: "A world without God would be a world without meaning."

He was immediately denounced for "making excuses" for the Church, ignoring clericalism, and not being tough on the clergy. But that last criticism runs against the facts. Once he became pope, he introduced severe penalties through a mechanism that forcibly laicized offending priests. This mechanism continues to be used by bishops with the determination to confront the lingering cases. Pope Francis embodied this discipline in Canon Law.

If the sexual revolution in this darkest area wreaked havoc within the Church, the mind boggles at the effects beyond the Church and Christian denominations. So much has been concealed in other institutions and communities, for example, the levels of sexual abuse of children among Indigenous Peoples in Australia and other nations.

The P Question

But what is pedophilia? We are confronted by a pathological condition that leads to criminal activity. Victims or survivors must receive compensation, support, counseling, and every possible healing service, but past failures and recent successes in this field should not detract from the critical question: *What causes a man or woman to act in this way?* Is this a mental illness? And why is it so often a *same-sex* activity?

The distinction between *being* a pedophile and *acting* as an abuser points to the need for remedial therapy, at least for the condition. Such therapy has been provided by some institutes. But the discussion remains unresolved about how effective various methods may be. The role of the sexual revolution is directly related to these questions. The sexual abuse of children has been with us always, a grim part of our fallen condition. But the obvious question remains: *Has the sexual revolution facilitated the spread of pedophilia?* Has this social revolution provided the ideal ambience for those who would harm those described by Our Lord as the "little ones" (Matthew 18:6)?

Legalizing Pedophilia?

Networking was revealed in the European and Asian pedophile rings, which were linked to international networks of child abusers. Nothing much has changed. But a wider and more sinister cover-up may be discerned.

In the outcry against child abuse within the Church, Christian denominations, and other religious communities, the memory of something dangerous has been conveniently forgotten—the *open existence of secular pedophile organizations*, such as the North American Man Boy Love Association. NAMBLA, and the British Paedophile Information Exchange, PIE. These networks promoted adult-child sexual relations in the United States and the United Kingdom and beyond, and they were linked to international networks. They have disappeared from view, but the pedophile rings survive as international police operations reveal, also networking on the "dark web". More importantly, the legislative goals of NAMBLA and PIE remain intact.

The descent toward legalizing the sexual abuse of children is made easier by:

- exaggerating the autonomous rights of the child;
- enabling children to make their own decisions about sex (child agency);
- denying parents' rights and their control of children;
- grooming children through internet pornography;
- grooming children with premature sex information that dissociates sex from love, fertility, and procreation;
- encouraging even small children to think that they are "gay";
- filling their heads with the confusing delusions of gender theory and ideology;
- enabling children to make their own decisions about changing their gender;
- and using puberty blockers to help achieve transition prior to surgery.

Moreover, returning to the LGBTQ+ spectrum, there is nothing to prevent P, for pedophile or pederast, from being added as yet another "gender". The ideologues coyly used "intergenerational sex", which may easily include such criminal activity.[4] Now they are using a bolder expression, **MAP**, meaning "minor-attracted persons", that is,

---

[4] A bizarre development is "kinder gender", when an adult "identifies" as a child, a more complex and dangerous delusion when combined with "trans-gender".

men and women who are attracted sexually to children. M would provide a place for pedophiles in the endless "diversity" of the gender spectrum.[5]

However, much evidence in the recent history of the sexual revolution shows that the pedophile cause can be traced back to at least 1977. A petition seeking to *remove all laws against sex between adults and minors* was signed by, among others, **Jean-Paul Sartre**, **Simone de Beauvoir**, and **Jacques Derrida**. The notable American radical poet **Allen Ginsberg** (1926–1997) was a pedophile who supported NAMBLA. The sexologist **Alfred Kinsey** and the psychologist **John Money** seemed sympathetic toward pedophilia. More recently, after the acceptance of **Judith Butler's** claim that "gender" is a fluid construct, the next step would be to accept her case for "child agency", that is, that children should make their own decisions about sexual activity, which is precisely what the pedophiles want.

Legal changes and policies that protect "child agency" suit those who want to groom, seduce, and abuse children. But the grooming of victims is already taking place wherever "safe schools" programs are established. Laced with the delusions of gender theory, these projects are being promoted and enforced by governments, usually on the Left, backed by think tanks, which in turn are well funded by governments or wealthy patrons. Parents and family groups who campaign to end these programs are denounced as bigots and enemies of free speech (!), the rights of the child, and civil liberties. They "offend" the experts.

However, outcry in the media from offended critics exposes the hypocrisy of the sexual Libertarians. They

---

[5] In August 2019, a "pedo-pride" group attempted to take part in the Gay Pride parade in Amsterdam. On February 29, 2020, an organization that brings together "gay children" and adults found a place in the annual Sydney Gay and Lesbian Mardi Gras.

caused the restraints to fall, and they want more restraints to fall. At the same time, they bewail the suffering of victims and signal their own virtues by castigating Christians and Jews for their past failures to confront pedophile crimes within faith communities. Yet the only argument secularists can muster against abusing children revolves around coercion and a lack of consent—which leads to the perverse conclusion that adult-child sexual relations may be good—if there is free consent! Once more, we are sliding back into the sleazy world of NAMBLA. This explains the subtle moves to reduce the age of consent so as to allow pedophile activity by a mutual free choice.

Is this terrible possibility the unfinished business of the sexual revolution?

8

Strategies to Bring Down
the Revolution

A s I INDICATED IN THE INTRODUCTION to this book,
even in the face of the massive influence and successes
of the sexual revolution, we should recognize the signs of
hope and the bright prospect of building the virtuous qualities of what Saint John Paul II called "the Civilization
of Love". This will also involve a struggle to reject and
reverse legislation that has virtually enforced the sexual
revolution in so many countries. At the same time, we
are called to work with compassion for the healing of the
men, women, and children whose lives have been ruined
by the sexual revolution.

Some Signs of Hope

In the early decades of the twenty-first century, we can
observe some signs of the fracturing of the sexual revolution because people are beginning to question its
achievements and look for more stable relationships. Most
people still favor fidelity in marriage. Adultery is popularly
described as "cheating".

One hopeful sign is the rejection of the **sexual
harassment of women** in the workplace, involving the

prosecution and shaming of male celebrities in politics, the media, and the arts and, along with these revelations, the exposure of some media celebrities who have abused children. Unfortunately, this trend has descended at times into "Me-too" witch hunts and the misuse of the law. But at least it indicates a return to some sense of sexual morality.

There is also a healthy revulsion against domestic violence. But what are the causes of this violence? Whether they are macho males or pathetic little bullies, the men who abuse women have been greatly encouraged by the sexual revolution. It provides them with fuel in the form of easily accessed pornography, violent and perverse electronic games, and the message that a man has the right to enjoy pleasure at the expense or pain of any woman. This violence can also be linked to what I claim is male control of the cohabitation game. Therefore, some feminists are recognizing that the sexual revolution is playing into the hands of men in the worst possible way.

Another area of the abuse and misuse of women is the surrogacy industry. This is now attracting attention as angry women and men in Asia and Africa strongly object to the exploitation of poor women. They are turned into incubators to provide babies for prosperous people in other countries, with the profit going to the operators.

"La Manif pour Tous"

A wider social and political change is already underway. In some countries, political instability has provoked a new movement. Some of us sense signs of an openness in favor of religion, decency, and family values.

In France, a critical moment was the *Manif pour tous* in February 2014, when huge crowds gathered in Paris and

Lyons to demonstrate *against* legalizing same-sex marriage. This came as a shock to the political establishment, Left and Right. The media tried to conceal these events by telling lies about the numbers who came onto the streets, when in fact this was the largest *manifestation* (protest demonstration) in French history.

Thanks to the *Manif pour tous* and subsequent silent youth protests, pro-marriage family networks continue to operate across a nation where a steady revival of faith is underway. This is linked to efforts to rediscover the Judeo-Christian roots of Western society and to resist attempts to rewrite the story of our culture by hating it and censoring it out of schools and universities. Even secularist politicians begin to ask whether we have lost "meaning" when we denigrate our cultural roots and faith-based values.

Therefore, if we look and listen carefully, we can welcome positive developments against permissiveness, for example:

- fathers making pledges to be faithful husbands,
- young women and men choosing to remain virgins until marriage,
- young women challenging older feminists,
- parents fighting bad sex-education programs and resisting the LGBTQ intrusion into schools,
- growing pro-family movements,
- movements to heal and strengthen marriage,
- young people admitting that they want marriage rather than just a string of "relationships",
- education in chastity, self-respect, and respect for others,
- education projects that affirm and honor Judeo-Christian ethics,
- projects to recover respect for Judeo-Christian culture,

- a gradual rise in vocations to a life of celibacy and chastity,
- imaginative modesty in dress and behavior.

Social conservatism may have some effects in the sexual domain. But, by itself, social conservatism cannot bring down the revolution. Ultimately, this is a spiritual struggle, good versus evil, light against darkness. At the heart of the confusion and flux, the Catholic Church is called to stand firm. Saint John Paul II, the courageous universal pastor, proclaimed a consistent and strong sexual ethic. He was hated by some, admired by others, and respected even by those who disagreed with him.

On the other hand, objective observers can see that *liberal Christianity is dying.* By contrast, conservative or traditional forms of Christianity are growing, and they appeal to the young. One reason for this trend is that they propose objective morality, particularly sexual ethics derived from the Scriptures and based on marriage, the family, and the virtues of chastity, self-respect, and self-control.

At the same time, young people who have been wounded by sexual immorality are seeking spiritual healing through an ordered Christian way of life based on an obedient faith in Jesus Christ. If we listen to their stories, we hear of decisive conversion experiences, not without suffering. Yet they teach us that self-sacrifice is possible, but only with the amazing grace of the Holy Spirit.

Permissive sexual Libertarians may denounce this trend as "fundamentalist", but their anger reveals insecurity. They vilify and mock anyone who questions their projects. But the promoters of the permissive society know that their revolution is threatened when family life, fidelity in marriage, and objective sexual morals become attractive once more, particularly among the young. Perhaps the collapse of Soviet Communism also weakened romantic attraction to the idea of "revolution". Nevertheless, the family remains the main target of the revolution. It is here, in this little critical battleground, that we must take our stand. It is here that we can fight for all families. This struggle calls for wise and subtle strategies.

A Twofold Strategy for Families

In our families, our parishes and schools, hence in our own lives, I propose two strategies for tackling the sexual revolution. At first sight, these ways seem to be different, but I believe we need both of them because they complement one another. I call one the *Benedictine Way*[1] and the other the *Yeast and Salt of the Kingdom*.

1. The Benedictine Way

In the golden ages of the expansion of the Church, monasteries for men and convents for women were strongholds of Christian faith and culture. In Europe and in the East, these religious communities pushed back paganism, resisted the violent inroads of Islam, and effectively counteracted ignorance and heresy. In the West, the supreme example of the monastic mission was the Benedictine tradition.

Religious communities formed and educated children and young people. They nursed the sick and the dying. They protected and fed the poor. They passed on a culture of art, music, literature, and learning. In a wide range of orders and congregations, their mission continues into our

---

[1] After I wrote this, I came across an excellent book applying a Benedictine way more widely: Rod Dreher, *The Benedict Option: A Strategy for Christians in a Post-Christian Nation* (New York: Sentinel/Penguin, 2017).

century, and we pray for more vocations. Now changes in society and the Church, not least the intrusion of the sexual revolution, call for the family to take up the mission of those religious communities. Is not the family the *domestic church*, the mini-church in the home?

Today, as never before, each Christian family must become a stronghold. Looking at this project as a "Benedictine Way" will involve "pulling up the drawbridge" and locking the doors and windows, which is what the monks and nuns did when the barbarians were at the gates. Parents need to be vigilant about who and what enters the home, through any "door" or "window"—for example, by way of children's access to the internet, their use of social media, or through associating with amoral people. Our Lord spoke of being strongly armed lest the thieves break in (Mark 3:27).

At the same time, parents need to be alert to certain risks. Locking out bad influences may become overly defensive, even obsessive. An overprotective parent may set up other problems, particularly unhealthy curiosity and reactive rebellion. Moreover, repressive Puritanism is not an authentic part of our Catholic traditions. Nor should we ever imply that the world "outside" is totally evil and that only our own circles are good.

Awareness of the presence of God and our need for God is essential in any good family. The Catholic understanding of the human person proposes that all of us are basically good, created in the beautiful image of God, yet we are "fallen", weak, and flawed, in need of the grace of divine forgiveness and conversion. Within families, the effects of this grace can be secured only when we draw on the means of grace: by worshipping together, by sacraments, shared prayer, and the reading of the Word of God. Changed by grace, we can come to understand ourselves and our own shortcomings, especially in the family context. One of the better effects of the social restrictions of the 2020 pandemic was a recovery of prayer in the home among many people of faith.

A sense of order is essential in any good family. Everyone should know "the rules", not as imposed, but understood as "our rules". So many parents tell me that children and young people want to know where they stand, what is permitted, and what is not permitted. Otherwise, a permissive message of so many free choices may set up deep anxiety. They need to know that there are boundaries. They need the security of knowing that there are also some protective "guardrails".

Particularly at puberty and adolescence, the young need to understand and identify the boundaries relating to appropriate behavior at home and outside the home, for example, questions regarding accountability, friendships, dating, the use of the internet, and their safety. *The reasons* for boundaries must be provided in a frank dialogue that begins with listening. It is never enough to fall back on "because I say so", which is a dangerous evasion of patient dialogue.

A sense of protective care is essential in any good family, but that can develop only if parents really know their children. So many parents have no idea where their children are, what they are doing or what company they are keeping. To provide care, supervision is essential. At the same time, let us bear in mind Saint Paul's wise words of caution: "Fathers, do not provoke your children to anger, but bring them up in the discipline and instruction of the Lord" (Ephesians 6:4).[2]

We notice that Paul refers to "fathers". The parenting role of the father is crucial. He can drive children away from religion, in the case of a tyrannical or godless father;

---

[2] See the advice of Pope Francis in *Amoris laetitia* (March 19, 2016), 260–73, "Where Are Our Children?"

on the other hand, by a humble example of prayer, he can ease the way for children to practice the faith later as adults.

A sense of humor is part of *joy*, one of the fruits of the Holy Spirit. In our families, it is useful to laugh at the sheer silliness of much of the sexual revolution, but without descending to cruel ridicule. It is also important to show young people that many promoters of sexual permissiveness lack a sense of humor, which is why their comedians can only fall back on obscenity and indecencies. They are often such joyless people.

The strong family also becomes a *place of healing and hope* for people denied a decent family life. So many families can attest to the way people are drawn to a home that is a true "domestic church" or a covenant-observant household. Here they discover how worshipping together, the sacraments and observances, the Word of God, and prayer shape our lives. Therefore, we need to appreciate that the Benedictine Way never means shutting morally wounded people out of our homes. When they knock on the door, they are seeking an atmosphere of security, safety, peace, joy, and a welcoming love that listens. They may not know it, but they are seeking the Lord God.

Therefore, in our lives, in our homes, we should cherish three priorities: *faith, family, and friends*. I learned this simple truth from two of my friends who are happy grandparents, John and Maureen. They speak from their experience of living the "good life" in a hospitable family of faith.

2. The Yeast and Salt of the Kingdom

The complementary way to the Benedictine approach is based on Jesus Christ calling Christians to be the "yeast" in the bread of society (see Matthew 13:33) and the "salt of the earth" that flavors that bread (see Matthew 5:13). Christ calls us, not to run away from the "wicked world" in reaction to its decadence, but rather to engage with the world.[3] A basic strategy is set before us. We are called, *not to be reactive, but to be proactive*. Where does effective action within society begin?

Beginning in the Family

The downside of reading this book is that some readers may feel daunted by the power in the sexual revolution. They may imagine they are helpless. That illusion should fade away once we take up the proactive approach by drawing on the resilient energies of the family and by working together.

Experience shows us that families make a difference when they come together. Collaborating and supporting one another, parents and grandparents, uncles and aunts, are energized as they become proactive in family associations, for example, in parents' groups, whether associated with schools or through home-schooling networks. An inspiring example is the *National Association of Catholic Families* (NACF), active in Britain and Australia.[4]

Mutual support not only builds up morale but sets up networks and strategies. Most importantly, the *illusion of isolation* fades away—

- *"Until I met this group, I thought we were the only traditional family in our area."*

---

[3] Because it reflects the active mission of the Dominican friars, this has been called the "Dominic Option".

[4] Contact: www.cfnews.org.uk and www.nacfaustralia.org.

- Then there is the positive feedback: *"We were at our wit's end until we discovered this family association ... it is so good to bring our children to beautiful events such as picnics for families."*
- And mutual support is welcomed: *"We have met wonderful, inspiring people here ... we have found new friends who really share our faith and morality ..."*
- Significantly, *"Here people listen to us and we can listen to them ..."*

But mutual support leads on to further action beyond the associations. I offer some practical examples because small organized groups or even a few committed individuals are being effective by forming or supporting local community circles:

- to close or keep out neighborhood sex shops and brothels;
- to expose bad sex-education programs in all schools;
- to challenge schools that promote gender diversity, transsexual experimentation, and child transitions;
- to ensure that contraceptives are not made available to teenagers;
- to ensure that abortion is not provided for teenagers;
- to expose those who fund the revolution;
- to expose those who profit from it;
- to use social media to promote truth and decency.

These activities should never be condescending ventures into a community but, rather, sincere engagement within a community. There is a need to be open to ecumenical and interfaith cooperation. The struggle is not a "Catholic thing" or an "Evangelical thing" or a "Jewish thing". And it must always be infused with prayer.

Better Education in Human Sexuality

One major battlefield is educating the young in the area of sexuality and fertility. Two rights predominate:

- the right of young children to innocence, hence appropriate timing;
- the right and duty of their parents to educate and form them, hence quality control.

Behind these issues, that crucial question arises again: *To whom does the child belong—to parents or the State?* As I have indicated, cultural Marxists and sexual Libertarians who prepare and enforce so much bad sex education do not believe that children belong to their parents. They despise and "deconstruct" the family. They do not believe in parental rights, and they mock a child's innocence.

When we provide children and young people with "the truth and meaning of human sexuality", we offer them clear moral guidance, not just some rules or slogans. For example:

- We help them to understand that there is objective moral truth, and so we form and cultivate their consciences and their self-respect.
- We make them aware of the dignity and uniqueness of their identity as males and females because sexuality is *being a woman and being a man.*
- We provide the biological "facts of life" gradually, at the appropriate stages of child and adolescent development.
- We always accompany this teaching with morality built around marriage and procreation.
- We train our children and young people to *see through* the deceit and delusions of the sexual revolution.

- We help them cultivate a critical understanding of the media, especially awareness of the dangers of being seduced and abused through the internet and social media.
- We help them to keep clear of the New Age swamp and to see through its superstitions, delusions, and moral decadence.

Good programs of education in human sexuality are available to be taken up by parents, parent groups, and schools working with parents. The fruit of the vision and medical and pastoral experience of Dr. Hanna Klaus, *Teen STAR*, is one remarkably successful program forming adolescents and young adults.[5]

Action Groups

Beyond the family circle, at the political level in the wider society, action groups have already challenged the sexual revolution and *always as an ecumenical endeavor*. When the sexual revolution first asserted itself in the United Kingdom, it was confronted by a housewife, **Mary Whitehouse** (1910–2001), who soon became a household name. For her attempts to clean up the media and retrieve censorship, she became a target of ridicule and misrepresentation, but she won support and respect across the nation, and she was honored by the Queen. Her work was promoted by British journalist **Malcolm Muggeridge** (1903–1990), who came to faith largely through Saint Teresa of Calcutta.

---

[5] Teen STAR contacts: teenstarprogram@gmail.com; Teen STAR, 2898 Mahan Drive—Suite 4, Tallahassee, Florida 32308; www.teenstar.org.

In the United States, the *Moral Majority* fought battles in the 1970s and '80s. *Family First, Focus on the Family,* and the *Eagle Forum* founded by **Phyllis Schlafly** (1924–2016)[6] have led families into "family politics", which inevitably includes confronting the forces and interest groups of the sexual revolution while working in the wider pro-life movement. In England, *Responsible Family* later became the *Family Education Trust,* an ecumenical think tank that takes on government at all levels on issues such as sex education and providing abortions and contraceptives for teenagers.[7]

Likewise, in Australia, Rev. **Fred Nile** (1934–) campaigned under the positive title *Festival of Light,* which later became a small, but effective, political organization that today operates as *FamilyVoice* Australia.[8] The *Australian Family Association*[9] and the *Endeavour Forum*[10] courageously engage in pro-life, pro-family politics and form activists and advocates.

Family politics means taking the initiative by getting "people of faith" to stand for election to public office. The ecumenical and interfaith approach is essential, and, whenever possible, formed and informed men and women should enter a range of political parties. The presence of people of faith is urgently needed at all levels of democratic political life, that is, in local, state, provincial, and national or federal legislatures. But to achieve this goal, we first need to dispel a purist mentality that politics is somehow "dirty". Those committed to advancing the

---

[6] The Family Education Trust: www.familyeducationtrust.org.uk.

[7] The Eagle Forum: www.eagleforum.org.

[8] FamilyVoice Australia, 4th Floor, 68 Grenfell St, Adelaide, SA 5000, Australia: www.familyvoice.org.au.

[9] Australian Family Association, 1401 Burke Rd, Kew East, Vic, 3102, Australia: www.family.org.au.

[10] Endeavour Forum: www.endeavourforum.org.au.

Judeo-Christian ethic must set aside such scruples and bravely set to work in society.

This raises the question of the place of public demonstrations, marches, and large gatherings. *La manif pour tous* worked well in France, where there is a well-established tradition of large public political events and demonstrations. Moreover, those who mobilized French Catholics carefully avoided control by the hard Right and concentrated on one issue. Likewise, the renowned *March for Life* in the United States brings together an ecumenical coalition of pro-life and pro-family movements and groups. These public events need to be focused and well planned, but also protected from disruption by vengeful activists or exploitation by fringe groups.

Fighting Sexual Exploitation

Another way is open to those committed to justice and the Judeo-Christian ethic—to take the initiative in taking on corrupt people who exploit other human beings sexually, especially through *sex-slavery* and *human trafficking*.[11] This is more specialized work. It has its dangers and risks. It opens some critical fields for action in support of vulnerable and marginalized women and men, young people, and children.

When I worked in the Vatican's Pontifical Council for the Family, I was entrusted with the task of coordinating an international conference in Bangkok on *child prostitution*. I also coordinated related conferences, on *street children*, in Rio de Janeiro, and on *child labor*, in Manila.

The conference of experts shook the Thai Government by focusing on the embarrassing scandal that large numbers

---

[11] See Pope Francis' encyclical *Fratelli tutti* (October 3, 2020), 24 and 38.

of child prostitutes of both sexes are exploited by "sex tourists" from the West. The conference recognized and honored those who rescue and rehabilitate these girls and boys, particularly those who lovingly nurse them when they are dying of AIDS. They are infected by male sex tourists who treat them as things for entertainment and pleasure, merely living sex toys to be used and then cast aside.

In Bangkok, we collaborated with the network *End Child Prostitution in Asian Tourism* (ECPAT). In those days, this nongovernmental organization was based in New Zealand. Now it has expanded into ECPAT International, based in Thailand and bringing together 103 organizations to fight all forms of sexual exploitation of children.[12]

Such areas of frontline work reflect the twofold social mission of the Catholic Church to promote moral truth, decency, and justice:

- by *internal reform*—cleaning up our own house first, and
- by *reaching out to cooperate with other Christians, members of other religions, and all people of goodwill.*

Let us work in a common cause to regenerate society and to rescue and heal the many victims of sexual exploitation.

[12] ECPAT International, Phayathai Road, Rachathewi, Bangkok, Thailand 10400: www.ecpat.org.

9

In the Light of Splendid Truths

THOSE WHO ARE THE SALT OF THE EARTH and the yeast of the kingdom are called to be a light to men and women in the world. This light does not come from us, for it is a gift, a grace from God. Amid the gloom and shadows described in this book, we are bearers of divine light, like candles shining brightly in the night. We may reflect on the old custom of handing a burning candle to the newly baptized or their parents at the celebration of baptism. And Jesus Christ encourages us, "Let your light so shine" (Matthew 5:16).

This is why our struggle against the sexual revolution should never be negative, aggressive, or destructive. What matters is not so much what we are "against" as, rather, what we are "for". Within the strategies suggested in the previous chapter is a precious treasury of vigorous spiritual and moral truths that permeate a culture of life and love. Without that Judeo-Christian heritage, even the best strategies are useless. By always drawing on the wisdom of that inspired scriptural heritage, our strategies can be effective.

Truth, Faith, and Reason

We do not seek to defeat anyone. Rather, we invite conversion. This is why I believe we should avoid using the term "culture wars", even while we know that this is a struggle between the *culture of life* and the *culture of death*. Our weapon is truth, but a warm truth that attracts, converts, encourages, heals, and inspires, the divine light that enlightens.

One of the great gifts of Saint John Paul II to the Church and the world was his encyclical letter *Veritatis splendor*, *The Splendor of the Truth* (1993). The inspiring first words of the letter provide a title that proclaims a simple message: the truth is always glorious. Truth is radiant with goodness and beauty. The moral truths we hold and try to live are imbued with these attractive qualities.

Moreover, in another encyclical letter, *Fides et ratio*, *Faith and Reason* (1998), Saint John Paul II showed how faith and reason work in harmony. In our struggle to bring down the sexual revolution, this is important to remember. A standard argument against us runs like this: "*but your views are just religious, matters of faith, the irrational fantasies of little 'people of faith'.*" Then they may resort to obscenities against us, words of anger, rage, for they are the ones who have lost the capacity to reason, to find peace, and to speak in peace. There is no peace in the sexual revolution.

Our calm response should be patient, positive, and rational. In the face of the new atheism and secularism, among Christians there is a revival of *apologetics*—the rational defense and explanation of our faith—and our morals. A new apologetics, envisioned by both the modern popes and evangelical leaders, must include a focused form of *ethical apologetics*, providing imaginative and reasoned arguments directed at refuting the errors and lies of the sexual revolution.

We are inspired by the call of Saint Peter: "*Always be prepared to make a defense to anyone who calls you to account for the hope that is in you, yet do it with gentleness and reverence; and keep your conscience clear, so that, when you are abused, those who revile your good behavior in Christ may be put to shame"* (1 Peter 3:15). He speaks to us from within the morally corrupt Greco-Roman world of the first century. His words resonate in our morally corrupt world of the twenty-first century.

Love and Sexuality

It is easy to see that something greater is lacking in the murky streams and reckless projects of the sexual revolution—*love.*

Faith and reason serve love. Permissiveness and promiscuity involve a failure to love, even a rejection of love. At the same time, this is a rejection of life. A sterile and heartless "civilization of death" has no place for love. It wages an endless war against what Saint John Paul II called the *"Civilization of Life and Love".*

Love is at the heart of "the truth and meaning of human sexuality". But what is "sexuality"? First and foremost, sexuality is the self-identity of *being a woman* and *being a man.* This is an essential part of the truth of the human person. Being a woman or man is a call to self-giving love. The vocation to love is why each of us has received the gift of life on this planet. The meaning of our lives is found in that vocation, that capacity to love.

A perceptive critic of postmodernity has pointed out that, while Saint Paul's popular hymn to love (1 Corinthians 13:1–3) is often sentimentalized, in reality Paul hits us with a tough challenge: "Without love, without the relation given to us as pure gift, it matters not what I do nor where I look. I am lost. I am nothing."[1]

---

[1] Conor Sweeney, *Abiding the Long Defeat: How to Evangelize like a Hobbit in a Disenchanted Age* (Brooklyn, N.Y: Angelico Press, 2018), p. 123.

Let us confidently use the *language of love*. This language is good, true, and it is always beautiful. Let us recover beautiful and powerful words. Let us teach these words to our children. Let us promote them in the media and raise them in prayer:

- Purity
- Decency
- Matrimony
- Chastity
- Virginity
- Celibacy
- Continence
- Fertility
- Procreation
- Purity of heart
- Harmony and peace of soul

Rediscovering Mystery and Intimacy

One theme closely related to love is the *mystery* of sexuality. A wise Catholic thinker, **Alice von Hildebrand** (1923–2022), consistently emphasized the need to recover the mystery of the nuptial relationship and femininity.[2] The sexual revolution has destroyed any sense of mystery in human sexuality. In debasing women and men, it cheapens, distorts, and demeans human sexuality, obviously through pornography. We need to recover the delicate beauty of a spiritual union and harmony of the body that is affectivity.

---

[2] Some useful books by Alice von Hildebrand are *The Privilege of Being a Woman* (2002) and *Man and Woman: A Divine Invention* (2010).

Affectivity can be discovered or recovered only by married couples themselves. Support groups and movements do help, such as *Marriage Encounter*. Yet they exist to encourage couples to rediscover mystery and intimacy as affectivity, making good marriages better and healing and rebuilding broken or damaged marriages. The marriage movements and sound counseling are rebuilding the culture of life and love, that positive response to the sexual revolution. Marriage movements also help couples rediscover what the sexual revolution erases—romance!

Christian Personalism

When it comes to human sexuality, there is a reasonable alternative to postmodern confusion and pessimism.[3] It offers an antidote to selfish individualism, and it is deeper than sugary subjectivism. This is the *Christian personalist* vision of man and woman, beautifully expressed in biblical terms in the *Theology of the Body* proposed by Saint John Paul II.

The personalist vision of sexuality is free from ugly tensions constructed by the mother of radical feminism, Simone de Beauvoir. As I have outlined, she reworked the Marxist class struggle as the struggle between the sexes or the "gender war", as they would describe it today. One of the tensions in that war is *suspicion*.

This personalist vision is free from the radical individualism of the postmodern society, which generates suspicion. My selfish "autonomy" reduces human sexuality by weakening or even destroying the essential quality of any good relationship—*trust*.

---

[3] See Appendix 3: The Problem with "Postmodern" Sex.

Because attitudes of suspicion and selfishness undermine trust, we must promote the rich relational principles such as:

- reverence for the body,
- celebrating the difference between females and males,
- promoting complementarity between the two sexes,
- rediscovering true intimacy.

Therefore, we need to cultivate these personal qualities in all marriages:

- self-giving love,
- self-sacrifice,
- communion,
- commitment,
- openness,
- mutual trust,
- affectivity and tenderness,
- shared decisions,
- sharing burdens,
- mutual respect,
- tolerating one another,
- forgiveness that forgets,
- openness to new life,
- loving care for every child as a unique person,
- reverence for and inclusion of elders,
- protection for the innocent,
- and forming a home that welcomes guests.

Let us reflect on all these "good things", encouraged by Saint Paul: "... *whatever is true, whatever is honorable, whatever is just, whatever is pure, whatever is lovely, whatever is gracious, if there is any excellence, if there is anything worthy of praise, think about these things*" (Philippians 4:8).

These lived qualities all depend upon *trust*. Put into practice, they cultivate and reinforce trust. They also offer the answer to that destructive sexual dualism, splitting the body from the mind or soul. The body is not an instrument to be used. The body is good and holy and is the means by which men and women make the self-gift in marriage. The self-gift is meant to be fruitful, life-giving. Yet we need a practical way to rise above another effect of this dualism, which relates to the issues around childbearing.

Natural Birth Spacing

Looking back across the history of the sexual revolution, we have seen that a decisive moment was the *separation of human sexuality from fertility*. One tiny object made the current phase of the sexual revolution possible, a technological breakthrough: the *contraceptive pill*.

In the decades leading to the invention and diffusion of the pill, Margaret Sanger and Marie Stopes were acting sincerely in their energetic "birth control" crusade. They wanted to assist poor women, to free them from the fear of pregnancy and the harm of multiple pregnancies. However, in their zeal, they did not see other consequences of separating lovemaking from having children, that is, of the temporary or permanent sterilization of a woman or a man.

They did not see that sterilized sexuality may reduce a woman or a man to a body that can be used and so easily exploited. By contrast, the body-soul unity is expressed in the capacity both to give life and to give love. *Life-giving and love-giving should never be torn apart.* If the body matters, the challenge today is to restore and strengthen a natural harmony between human sexuality and fertility, to bring love-giving and life-giving together again. This applies to both women and men.

The practical way forward is available in the various modern methods of fertility awareness, when couples discover the natural cycle in a woman's body and use it *either to achieve or to postpone pregnancy*. Let us never describe these methods as "natural family planning" or "fertility control", language that echoes a modern demand always to be in control, to plan, to determine.

I was a good friend and disciple of the two great experts in this field, Dr. John Billings (1918–2007) and Dr. Lyn Billings (1918–2013). They also taught me that awareness of fertility in the natural cycles leads to a more intimate and tender sexual relationship. Husband and wife come together and share decisions as equals, and so they deepen their married love. This contradicts what people imagine about natural methods. Attacks on the methods focus on the abstinence required to postpone pregnancy. We note the shallow assumption of the sexual revolution that self-control is wrong or even harmful. At the same time, there are also some wider benefits of natural methods in terms of women's rights and justice.

Mother Teresa's sisters teach natural birth spacing to the poorest of the poor. They strengthen the health of these women and free them from a subservient role in marriage. As they map their cycles, women are empowered with knowledge that challenges male demands and the macho domination that poisons certain cultures.

How strange it is that we explore and understand the mysteries of outer space, and yet most women know very little about the "inner space" of their own fertility. Do not all women on earth have a right to this knowledge? The big pharmaceutical companies do not want them to have that knowledge. Natural methods cost virtually nothing.

Contraception involves big money. Here we have another exploitative effect of the sexual revolution.

However, within the Catholic Church, there is need to overcome a mood of indifference. Time has passed. It is over half a century since Saint Paul VI favored natural spacing of births in *Humanae vitae* 24 and 27, later promoted by Saint John Paul II in *Familiaris consortio*, 32–35. Two Synods of Bishops on the Family (2014 and 2018) and the papal exhortation *Amoris laetitia* (2016) endorsed this way forward, but no practical guidelines have appeared and the dedicated teachers of the methods have had little encouragement.

This was a lost opportunity but no surprise to me. Some bishops do not have a clue about natural birth spacing and what it means in marriage. By contrast, other bishops in developing countries are aware of what it offers women and the justice issues involved, particularly when Planned Parenthood arrives with its menu of abortions, contraceptives, and sterilizations. Yet here a deep moral challenge faces the shepherds of the Christian flock. If we pastors do not offer couples a way to live Church teaching, we are no better than the lawyers denounced by Christ for laying burdens on people's shoulders without raising a finger to lift them (see Matthew 23:4).

Virtues Education

We need education and formation to present the truths we pass on to our children, grandchildren, nieces, and nephews. For Catholics, the great source and ultimate resource is the *Catechism of the Catholic Church*, in particular part 3, *Life in Christ*, which covers human nature, law, grace, and the Ten Commandments. The *Catechism* approach is in harmony with what Bible-believing Christians and observant Jews hold when we all face the challenges of the sexual revolution.

Reading part 3 of the *Catechism*, we should note the positive approach, that the highest moral qualities or "virtues" come before delineating the sins. Although we are fallen weak beings, needing grace, we can find in God's commandments a way to live the virtues, to become virtuous people. The virtues counteract the sexual revolution by establishing good moral habits in our daily lives, particularly as we relate to other people and make moral choices. But what are these virtues?

The supernatural virtues are faith, hope, and love (charity). These greatest virtues come from God as a free gift of grace, so they are described as "supernatural" or "theological".

The cardinal virtues are prudence, justice, temperance, and fortitude. The word "cardinal" comes from the Latin word for a hinge, because these virtues are four "hinges" on which a good moral life depends.

Therefore, in our own lives and in what we teach children and young people, we need to cultivate respect for and knowledge of:

- the virtues, supernatural and cardinal,
- the Ten Commandments,
- Christ's New Commandment to love,
- the Beatitudes,
- the Natural Law,
- conscience as moral judgment,
- formation of conscience.

However, forming one's conscience involves what Saint Ignatius of Loyola called the *discernment of spirits*. We need to be "as wise as serpents and as innocent as doves"

(Matthew 10:16). Wisdom helps us discern what is a right path and what is a wrong path in life.

Moral Integrity with Some Cautions

The word "integrity" is useful in helping us to discern what makes a person morally strong, armed for the struggle of life. An integrated person keeps together moral qualities that gradually build up a strong character. Here are some of them:

- decency, in thought, word, deed, and appearance;
- self-respect with a healthy level of self-love;
- a sense of dignity;
- yet humble, without pride or pretense;
- duty, to God and to others;
- duty to one's nation;
- truthfulness, in speech and intention;
- avoiding a "double life";
- taking responsibility for one's actions;
- courage in confronting what is wrong;
- enduring abuse and vilification;
- moderation in life-style: food, drink, comforts ... ;
- treating others with fairness;
- listening to others with patience;
- maintaining respect for others, and
- always relying on the amazing grace of God.

These are some of the concrete ways that help us live according to those cardinal virtues: *prudence, justice, temperance,* and *fortitude.* However, this framework for moral integrity must never become a source of pride. We should be careful to avoid *"virtue signaling".* This is a subtle form of hypocrisy. Unfortunately, sending signals such as *"Look, how wise and good we are!"* has become the smug expression of political correctness and the superiority of the "woke" people.

Never Look Back

In resisting the sexual revolution, we need to avoid another subtle temptation, *nostalgia*, looking back wistfully to better times. This applies first to older people, who may yearn for the "good old days", wishing that the "happy days" could return, even imagining that they can return. While some people remember an era when there was no sexual revolution and family life was stable, I would advise them to reflect on the disturbing historical details set out in the first chapters of this book. What appeared to be tranquil was turbulent beneath.

The projects, ideologies, and misguided thinkers of a sexual revolution were already at work. Certain social questions had to be resolved in the decades after the Second World War, the era of postwar reconstruction, migrations, postcolonial development, the Cold War, geopolitical changes, new media technology, etc. The issues revolved around the role of women, the rights of minorities, and concerns about population and ecology, running into the new century with the challenges of the post-9/11 focus on terrorism and then the economic crisis of the post-COVID era. None of this can be ignored as it shapes our world, but so much of it has been exploited by the agents of the sexual revolution, working away in the long march of the current cultural revolution.

We are also called to look forward confidently, beyond whatever afflicts our families in these times. In each home, we can quietly build the little communities of a new society, glowing with the culture of life and love. But the good families of the future will not be the same as those in some idealized past. Nostalgia may distract us, even as we can quietly restore many good things, but "restorationism" is not enough. The hand once set on the plow[4] impels us to go forward and not to look back.

Living the Good Life

Because we are responding to the perennial challenge, *"How then should we live?"* we are not considering abstract ideas. We are concerned with what happens in our daily life in this world. Therefore, we need the examples of those remarkable men and women who have led good lives. Inspiring and attractive role models are essential for all of us. Above all, the lives and witness of these saints can encourage and inspire the young:

- Saint Agnes and Saint Agatha, virgins and martyrs,
- Saint Aloysius Gonzaga and Saint Dominic Savio, patrons of youth,
- Saint Thérèse of Lisieux, virgin and Doctor of the Church,
- Saint Gemma Galgani, virgin and mystic,
- Saint Maria Goretti, virgin and martyr,
- Saint José Sanchez del Rio, young soldier and martyr,
- Blessed Pier Giorgio Frassati, patron of youth,
- Saint Gianna Beretta Molla, mother and patron of unborn human life,
- Saints Louis and Zélie Martin, parents of Saint Thérèse,
- Blessed Carlo Acutis (1991–2006), first candidate for sainthood of the millennial generation.

---

[4] See Luke 9:62. A rich resource for faith, culture, and society is *Plough*, a magazine published quarterly in print and weekly online: plough.com/en.

Let us always seek what they sought in their virtuous lives of purity and integrity. By God's grace, they held firmly to whatever is *good, true, and beautiful* ... because what the sexual revolution has unleashed among the young is not good; it is untrue, and it is always ugly.

Spiritual Weapons, Angelic Armor

We carry within us the effects of Original Sin; we are all weak, sinful, and vulnerable. Every day, various forms of the media throw out images and messages that can cause temptations. All those saints named above had to struggle with temptations and distractions during their lives on planet Earth. In dealing with our own day-to-day struggles and in helping others, we must always remember that *all sexual sins can be forgiven*, even the worst excesses promoted by the sexual revolution.

The spiritual warrior stumbles and falls only to rise again and fight. This message of hope was beautifully captured by Saint Paul. Writing to the faithful in the sleazy seaport of Ephesus, he points to the image of an armed Roman soldier of his time. He urges us to put on spiritual armor: truth around our waist, righteousness as our breastplate, peace for our footwear, faith as a shield that deflects the flaming darts of the devil, along with the helmet of salvation, but above all, in our hand is the sword of the Spirit, which is the Word of God (see Ephesians 6:10–17).

When we need power and protection, the spiritual weapons and angelic armor are always at hand. The armory I propose comes out of my own tradition, but it can be adapted by other people of faith:

- A spirit of "prayer and penance",
- Prayer, fasting, and alms for the poor,

- Penitence, making a good confession,
- Regular Holy Communion,
- Devotion to the Blessed Sacrament,
- Daily self-examination of conscience,
- Being nourished by reading the Scriptures,
- Meditating on the mysteries of the Rosary,
- Prayer to the ever-Virgin Mother of God,
- Finding stillness and silence,
- Keeping your heart set on the goal of eternal life.

These divine gifts arm and protect us on the journey, but they also put order into our lives. An *ordered life* is the good alternative to the disordered lives of those who are imprisoned by the sexual revolution.

That ordered life is marked by what we all can seek and achieve:

- purity of heart and mind,
- chastity, based on self-control,
- self-sacrifice,
- the choice of chastity and fidelity in relationships,
- ascetical discipline,
- keeping custody of what I see,
- control of what I hear,
- decency in speech,
- grace in time of temptation.

Pastoral Action

I have emphasized the need to offer healing and hope to the many victims of the sexual revolution. It is useful to list practical actions. In concrete terms, we can do much for them by:

- providing sound counseling, offered with patience,
- not preaching, but walking with them,
- never being shocked or "offended",
- always offering encouraging words of hope,
- suggesting strategies to plan an ordered life,
- introducing those who are confused to wise and faithful friends.

There is so much we can do to heal and rebuild the bruised lives of men, women, and children. This is most important because the sinister gender war against the body is producing ever more victims. Many of them need professional help. A fine center of pastoral ministry to the survivors of the sexual revolution is the Ruth Institute founded by Jennifer Roback Morse.[5]

The Cosmic Struggle

We return to the beauty of moral truth shining in the light of the three great civilizing principles: *what is good, what is true,* and *what is beautiful.* The sexual revolution is contrary to all that is good. It destroys truth with lies and deceit. It erases beauty because it rejoices in ugliness. These drastic inversions impel us to discern and identify its real source: *evil.*

In the Gospels and the Acts of the Apostles, we read that Jesus Christ and his apostles did not hesitate to exorcise "unclean spirits".[6] The diabolical factor in the impurity and lust of the sexual revolution cannot be ignored, nor

---

[5] The Ruth Institute, 4845 Lake Street, Suite 217, Lake Charles, Louisiana 70605. www.ruthinstitute.org.

[6] For example, Luke 4:36, Matthew 10:1, Mark 1:27, 6:7.

can it be explained away. This is not only a culture war or some competition between "value systems". Rather, it is part of the great cosmic struggle, the perennial conflict between the luminous kingdom of God and the gloomy domain of our foe, Satan. The "kindly Light" that leads us is opposed to a satanic darkness that engulfs and chokes us. This struggle with evil enters our daily lives in this world, and so much evil has been unleashed by the sexual revolution. Yet we have a champion, the warrior archangel, Saint Michael, who defends us from evil in the day of battle.

We Need Saints

What, then, does our world need as we come face to face with evil? Above all, this world needs holy souls—men, women, and children who are wise and courageous, not easily deceived, but strong and effective light bearers. As Jesus Christ said, they are called to be "as wise as serpents and as innocent as doves" (Matthew 10:16).

We also have a biblical promise regarding wisdom: "In every generation she passes into holy souls and makes them friends of God" (Wisdom 7:27). One of those souls is Saint Teresa Benedicta Stein (1891–1942). Edith Stein was a German philosopher who became a Carmelite nun after her conversion. This Jewish martyr and mystic speaks to us in our tangled times. Across the years, out of the darkness of the Nazi tyranny that murdered her at Auschwitz, we hear her affirming that:

> *The more an era is engulfed in the night of sin and estrangement from God,*
> > *the more it needs souls united to God.*
> > *And God does not permit a deficiency.*

The greatest figures of prophecy and sanctity step forth out of the darkest night.

But, for the most part, the formative stream of the mystical life remains invisible. Certainly the decisive turning points in world history are substantially co-determined by souls whom no history book ever mentions.

And we will only find out about those souls to whom we owe those decisive turning points in our personal lives on the day when all that is hidden is revealed.

The Hidden Life
ICS Publications, Washington, D.C., 110

The Future

Is the sexual revolution permanent? Is it just another social "swing" that affects only some countries? Could it be followed by a swing to the opposite extreme?

We should be cautious when trying to answer such speculative questions. This swing to permissiveness is larger and more pervasive than any behavioral shift in human history, and, in a globalized world, it is not limited to a few countries. Big money, modern communications, clever propaganda, ideology, and the politicization of sex through legislation have turned the revolution into an institution. Broadly considered, this institution is powerful, rich, and apparently successful and well established. But when a revolution becomes an institution, the forces against it themselves become "revolutionary", and that is our advantage.

APPENDIX 1

Where to Find the Teaching of the Catholic Church on Human Sexuality

Sources

- Pope Pius XI, encyclical letter, *Casti connubii*, 1930: this letter on marriage included the pope's response to the Anglican surrender on contraception at the 1930 Lambeth Conference.
- Pope Pius XII, various discourses on specific issues, such as the *Address to Italian Midwives*, 1951, and the *Address to Directors of Associations for Large Families*, 1958; encyclical letter, *Sacra virginitas*, 1954, reaffirming the higher vocation to celibacy and virginity for the Kingdom.
- The Second Vatican Council, *Pastoral Constitution on the Church in the Modern World, Gaudium et spes*, 1965, nos. 47–52: this teaching on marriage as a holy covenant and the Christian family also foreshadowed the teaching on birth control.
- Pope Saint Paul VI, encyclical letter, *Humanae vitae*, 1968: repeating and clarifying the Church's teaching against contraception, sterilization, and abortion, and at the same time affirming a strong doctrine of love and life in marriage.
- Congregation for the Doctrine of the Faith, *Persona humana, Declaration on Certain Questions of Sexual*

Ethics, 1975: a succinct statement on specific sexual sins and problems, also to resolve doubts raised by dissenting theologians.

- Pope Saint John Paul II, post-synodal apostolic exhortation, *Familiaris consortio*, 1982: especially useful for teaching on marriage and the personalist development of *Humanae vitae*.

- Congregation for the Doctrine of the Faith, *Letter to the Bishops on the Pastoral Care of Homosexual Persons*, 1986: prudent pastoral guidance on a growing problem.

- Congregation for the Doctrine of the Faith, *Donum vitae, Instruction on Respect for Human Life in Its Origin and on the Dignity of Procreation*, 1987: relevant to sexual ethics as it deals with the other side of the harm caused once the unitive and procreative dimensions of sexual union are willfully separated.

- Pope Saint John Paul II, encyclical letter *Veritatis splendor*, 1993: the most important foundational document insofar as it proposes objective morality and rules out situational ethics, proportionalism, and consequentialism, theories that have weakened sexual ethics among Christians.

- Pope Saint John Paul II, *Gratissimam sane, Letter to Families*, 1994: this includes statements of teaching on marriage and procreation.

- Pope Saint John Paul II, encyclical letter *Evangelium vitae*, 1995: relevant to our subject because it includes teaching on abortion and contraception.

- Pope Saint John Paul II, encyclical letter *Fides et ratio*, 1998: relevant to our subject because it includes teaching on faith and reason.

- Pope Francis, post-synodal apostolic exhortation *Amoris laetitia*, 2016: no. 56, rejecting gender ideology and practices.

The Catechism of the Catholic Church is the authoritative source where these teachings are brought together. The following sections should be noted because they can form the basis for answers to problems when preparing educational programs and student resources:

- male and female sexual identity, nos. 355, 369–73, 1605, 2331–36;
- the sacrament of marriage, nos. 1601–58;
- accepting one's male or female sexual identity, nos. 2332–33;
- the sixth commandment and chastity, nos. 2337–50;
- sins against chastity, nos. 2351–59;
- married love and fidelity, nos. 2360–65;
- procreation, nos. 2366–79;
- sins against marriage, nos. 2380–91;
- the ninth commandment and purity, nos. 2514–27.

Succinct statements derived from the above paragraphs can be found in a question-and-answer format in the *Compendium of the Catechism of the Catholic Church* authorized by Pope Benedict XVI.

Other More Recent Documents

The Pontifical Council for the Family prepared some useful applications of the teaching of the Church in specific related fields:

- *Preparation for the Sacrament of Marriage*, 1996, guidelines for the several stages of preparing people for marriage.
- *Vademecum for confessors concerning some aspects of the morality of conjugal life*, 1997, a pastoral guide for priests.

- *Family, Marriage, and "de facto" Unions*, 2000, on the issues involved in the widespread practice of cohabitation.
- *The Family and Human Procreation*, 2006, places the issues in a positive sense amid the challenges of the "postmodern" era of the twenty-first century.

APPENDIX 2

Where to Find Catholic Teaching on Education in Human Sexuality

The Church promotes and regulates the Christian formation of young people in human sexuality. This constant pastoral and catechetical concern is guided by the key documents for parents and those who assist them.

- Pope Pius XI, *Divini illius magistri*, 1929; on the education of youth.
  The pope responds to the emergence in Scandinavia, Germany, and the Soviet Union of "value-free" sex education. Largely in the light of this encyclical, Catholic schools began to introduce cautious and modest forms of education in sexuality.

- The Second Vatican Council, *Declaration on Catholic Education, Gravissimum educationis*, 1965.
  In the foundational sections of this Declaration, the Council Fathers call for a "positive and prudent" education in sexuality. This could be fleshed out only in the years after the council.

- Pope Saint John Paul II, *Familiaris consortio*, 1981.
  Developing what the Second Vatican Council had indicated and responding to requests and proposals from bishops and experts at the Synod of Bishops on the Family, 1980, the pope adds "clear and delicate"

to "positive and prudent" as qualifying phrases for education in human sexuality. He spells out the rights and corresponding duties of parents, the primary educators in this field. He maintains the concern of previous popes to avoid sliding into secularist "sex education".

- The Congregation for Catholic Education, *Educational Guidance in Human Love*, 1983.
  This guide was prepared mainly for Catholic schools as a way of offering a better perspective on human love for education in human sexuality, so as to avoid a purely biological and "value-free" approach that became the source of problems, not only in public schools, but in some Catholic schools. The document begins by reaffirming the principles of *Familiaris consortio*, that is, the need to respect and honor the primary educative role of parents.

- The Pontifical Council for the Family, *The Truth and Meaning of Human Sexuality*, 1995.
  Published at the direction of Pope Saint. John Paul II to complement, complete, and balance the previous document, this is the most recent authoritative source. Building on all previous sources, it provides not only guidance for parents in forming their children in the home, but also one of the most extensive summaries and applications of Church teaching on sexuality. The principle of subsidiarity runs throughout the document, based on the natural right and role of parents who can do so much as the first educators called to take up this work. It provides a detailed guide to all who work in this field, not only parents, but all others who assist them, such as teachers, etc.

- Pope Francis, *Amoris laetitia* (2016), 280–86.
  Based on previous guidelines, in the family context of chapter 7, *On the Better Education of Children*, the pope maintains the need to provide solid education in human sexuality as a challenge facing Catholic institutions.

- The Congregation for Catholic Education, *Male and Female He Created Them*, 2019.
  These guidelines for schools affirm the reality and beauty of sexual difference, setting out the Catholic rejection of gender fluidity and gender ideology and a dualistic understanding of the person. Pastoral ways are proposed to foster dialogue and help the young to grow up free from gender confusion.

- Pontifical Council for Promoting the New Evangelization, *Directory for Catechesis*, 2020, 373–78.
  Principles of bioethics and teachings on the male-female sexual difference are set out as the template for catechesis and religious education. While pastoral care is envisaged, the postmodern ideology that reduces gender identity to a social construction is rejected, hence it cannot be taught in Catholic schools.

APPENDIX 3

The Problem with "Postmodern" Sex

The postmodern approach to sex is not easy to define. As I have explained, in the postmodern culture all truth is relative and merely words, so "narratives" are to be deconstructed. In that mind-set, the permissive approach to sex prevails. As already indicated, this trend is supported by an extreme individualism, *autonomy*, which has been criticized as a destructive characteristic of Western liberal societies by Saint John Paul II, Benedict XVI, and Pope Francis.

However, bringing together sex and reason is no simple exercise. To demonstrate that the postmodern attitudes to sex are irrational is likewise not so simple, for within a postmodern framework, sexual relationships might be set out in a kind of self-contained rational way, that is, as transient, temporary but practical arrangements that satisfy human desires and needs. The practice of relativism prevails once you deconstruct language and reality.

The old irrational approach to sex, or, to put it better, the nonreasonable approach, stemmed from several sources, principally the romantic movement, leading to the view that sex is all about feelings and passions—so sex is too hot for reason. There is some truth in this, as Saint Thomas Aquinas calmly observed. Obviously, human sexuality involves affectivity, emotions, and passion. A purely rational approach to sex can be as nonsensical as a totally romantic approach. This is why I prefer to speak of a "reasonable" approach, a well-thought-out approach, for example by first taking into account other people and not just focusing on myself and "my needs".

I would suggest that those who apply such a reasoned approach to sex today are usually religious-minded people. Being reasonable about sex can hose down much postmodern sexual behavior by showing that it is irresponsible and harmful, especially to women, children, and the family. But to *take responsibility* is exactly what the postmodern philosophers will never do. The wider culture they influence or echo is irresponsible, reckless, callous, and cruel, without any sense of shame.

The old existentialists were on better ground here. Indeed, some of them described the defining human experience as *taking responsibility*, being decisive, making a commitment. Jean-Paul Sartre might have looked the other way when the Germans marched into Paris in 1940, but other existentialists made a decision to resist evil, often at great cost. Those twentieth-century existentialists retained much of the old Judeo-Christian ethic, with its reasoned framework of always taking other people into account, which is a natural basis for commitment, providing the balance for a healthy individualism.

INDEX